Marketer of the Day

Insights from the Top Internet Marketers & Entrepreneurs Around the World

Compiled by Robert Plank
www.MarketerOfTheDay.com

All rights reserved. No part of this publication may be reproduced or transmitted in any form or by any means, electronic or mechanical, including photocopy, recording or any information storage and retrieval system, without prior permission in writing from the publisher.

© 2019 by JumpX LLC, (408) 277-0904

Introduction 1

Chapter 1: Simple Is Better Than Incomplete by Robert Plank 5

Chapter 2: The Perfect Day Formula by Craig Ballantyne 23

Chapter 3: Search Engine Optimization, Content Marketing, Pinterest and YouTube by Kellen Kautzman 35

Chapter 4: Transition to the Next Stage of Your Life by Terri Rose 49

Chapter 5: Parse Your Story to Meet Your Audience by Jeanne Alford 61

Chapter 6: Live Long and Stay Productive At Any Age by Renee Balcom . 71

Chapter 7: Break Outside Your Comfort Zone by Philip Williams 83

Chapter 8: Build an Online Business Through Content Marketing by Bernie Thompson 93

Chapter 9: Write Your Book in a Flash by Dan Janal 101

Chapter 10: Get That Consistent Stream of New Leads by Joe Kashurba 113

Chapter 11: Create a Great Customer Experience by Kenneth Bator 121

Chapter 12: Goals, Finances, Budgeting & Growth by Ruby Tan 129

Chapter 13: Create, Qualify and Close Phone Leads by Glen Shelton 135

Chapter 14: Make Money Using Raw Land by Mark Podolsky 143

Chapter 15: Done For You Product Launches, Lead Capture & Conversion by Larry Becht 153

Chapter 16: Task and Project Management Using Asana, PipeDrive & Slack by Paul Minors 159

Chapter 17: Become Your Best Self and Discover Your Aligned Life Roadmap by River Easter 167

Conclusion 175

Introduction

What do the world's top thought leaders, business owners, human beings have in common? Those that have broken through, put themselves out there, and discovered a system that works... what did they do correctly that others failed at? You're about to find out!

- **Robert Plank** explains how to keep things simple, get ugly early, avoid self-sabotage, and ramp up.

- **Craig Ballantyne** can help you with unhappiness and procrastination, showing how you can regain control and that freedom equals discipline.

- **Kellen Kautzman**, content marketer, explains the strategy of generating useful information and shows you how to model the success of top YouTube and Instagram stars.

- **Terri Rose**, love and lifestyle coach, has made it her mission to get you to experience positivity and see things differently through journaling, mantras, self-care, group support, and so much more.

- **Jeanne Alford** is a Public Relations communication expert who can help you to customize your presentation, use metaphors, calm down, and most importantly, listen.

- **Renee Balcom** is a community health worker who has helpful tips on getting everything done, living to an old healthy age, and keeping your quality of life at its best.

- **Philip Williams** is a consultant who provides excellent advice on how to remind yourself of your greatest life accomplishments, change your company culture, and examine your past successes/failures to live the best life possible.

- **Bernie Thompson** is an inventor who wants you to innovate, explain, and make your business fun again.

- **Dan Janal** is the go-to expert when it comes to writing your book in a flash, who shares a few strategies, techniques, and mind-hacks to getting your thoughts onto paper quickly... by creating your content OUT OF order.

- **Joe Kashurba** is a wizard when it comes to landing web design clients, and he explains how you can stand out in any profession, as well as how to avoid becoming a "slave" to any of your clients.

- **Kenneth Bator** has over 15 years of experience providing excellent customer experiences, and he's all about asking probing questions to dive deep, arrive at logical conclusions, and set service standards to achieve consistent results in business AND life.

- **Ruby Tan** is a bookkeeper who tells you what you need to know to slash expenses and avoid poverty in all areas of life... by planning ahead, adhering to a few simple rules, and working SMARTER instead of harder.

- **Glen Shelton** runs a call center and explains his thought process when it comes to building a team, pivoting to new markets, and debugging the system for maximum results.

- **Mark Podolsky**, raw land geek, has a very interesting passive income system that he's used to live life on his own terms, and he reveals how you can fill a need AND follow a proven, repeatable system, to follow in the footsteps of others.

- **Larry Becht** specializes in ClickFunnels: namely, done-for-you landing pages and product launches. He dispenses excellent advice when it comes to consolidating your various online systems and making the most out of proven marketing tools.

- **Paul Minors** is a productivity genius who can help you get a handle on your task and project management, but he realizes that software is not a magical solution, so he provides an easy way to get your organization to adopt proven solutions.

- **River Easter** is a mind master whose mission in life is to get you to overcome self-doubt, smart small, create winning goals, love what you do, and find your gratitude.

You probably already know that you need outside help to get fresh perspectives, renewed motivation, and to get to where you need to go in business and life. You're probably also aware that success stories, tales of overcoming obstacles, and expert advice is incredibly helpful to overcome the usual negative "head trash" that comes along with settling, compromising, giving up, and doubting yourself.

Pay close attention to those people that have traveled the path you want to take. Absorb the excellent advice (and stories) that come from the experts in the *Marketer of the Day!*

If You Like This Book, Please Leave a Review:

MarketerOfTheDayBook.com/amazon

**It will be greatly appreciated.
We would love to hear your feedback.**

Chapter 1: Simple Is Better Than Incomplete by Robert Plank

When was the last time you made life way too hard on yourself? (Maybe you only realized it in hindsight.)

Leonardo da Vinci once said, "Simplicity is the ultimate sophistication." Or maybe, when it comes to your business, your career or your job -- if you can't explain it to a 5-year-old, then you don't understand it yourself!

The less choices you must make, the better. Studies have shown that the most successful people wake up early, exercise, drink lots of water and practice good sleeping habits.

In high school, I visited a friend who was working a summer job. He was being paid to install Microsoft Office (Word, Excel, etc.) on 60 different school computers. They expected him to sit down at computer #1, pop in a CD-ROM, click through screen after screen, wait 45 minutes, then eject the disc and move on to the next computer.

I walked into the room. He was installing the software on ALL 60 computers at once. All 60 computer screens in the room showed 22% progress, then 23%, then 24%. These computers were networked, and he had found an article online showing how to "stream" the installation of this software onto all 60 computers at once. To paraphrase Bill Gates, "If I want something done, I'll hire a lazy person to do it, because he'll find an easy way to do it."

Simpler and Shorter Is Better

My perspective was forever changed one day in history class in high school, when I learned about Abraham Lincoln's Gettysburg Address, which was delivered four months after the ending of the American Civil War. Just before Lincoln's speech at Gettysburg, Edward Everett delivered a 2-hour speech -- completely normal for a cemetery dedication at that time. However, President Lincoln was not feeling well, and HIS speech only lasted two minutes, only ten sentences. Nonetheless, Lincoln's speech is the one that went down in history. The lesson I learned that day was you can sometimes make more of an impact by being concise.

French mathematician Blaise Pascal had a saying, "I have made this letter longer than usual because I had not had time to make it shorter." It made perfect sense: whatever I had to say could be said in fewer words. Imagine having two books on a table in front of you. Both contain the exact same information, but one is 300 pages and the other is only 30 pages long. Exact same information. Which is more helpful? Answer: the book that gives you what you need in 10% of the time.

A common reason for failure: the trap of hiding behind complexity. I can only speak for myself, but when I've experienced stress, overwhelm, analysis paralysis or cognitive dissonance (holding two conflicting beliefs), it was usually because I needed to reduce the clutter in my life.

You may have heard of the story of Isaac Newton watching an apple fall from a tree in order to "realize" his theory of gravity. Legend has it that, thousands of years ago, Archimedes was tasked by King Heiro of Syracuse (Sicily) to differentiate gold from other metals without melting them down. As Archimedes lowered himself into a bathtub, he noticed the water rising. This was Archimedes' "Eureka Moment" that led to measuring the density of metals based on the water they displaced... an easy way to differentiate pure gold from other metal coins.

Another life changing moment was being a kid and visiting my grandfather, who lived until age 95 and had worked for NASA and JPL on space missions. I was very puzzled when I found a mysterious 10-page document stapled to the refrigerator in his garage. It was a bullet-pointed to-do list of to-do lists. Lists of tasks to clean up the garage, improvements to the garden, things to be done on the car, etc. I was overwhelmed just paging through it!

It was at that point I realized my own shortcomings. Every single one of us has fallen into the trap of making the most beautifully laid plans, the most detailed and revised document that outlines the absolute perfection our business and life could take if only we implemented. The all-too-common problem: using up all the time you would have spent COMPLETING that task on PLANNING the task. Not good.

Suggestion #1: You Only Have Enough Bandwidth for Four Tasks Every Day

Let's keep things sustainable for you. I imagine that you've pulled an all-nighter at some point in your life or raced against the clock to finish an assignment in time. It wasn't very fun OR fulfilling, was it? Unfortunately, people today live in that same cycle of procrastination and then desperation... racing to pay the bills, get out of debt, turn in those assignments on time, etc.

Bad habits are to blame. Not only the obvious like multitasking, developing a habit for distraction (smartphones and social media), bad time management or lack of follow-through. The REAL bad habit comes from having your priorities out of order.

No one on Earth can get more than 24 hours out of any day. Once you subtract the need for 8 hours of sleep and 8 hours of relaxation, you're left with 8 working hours. However, if you've worked for long periods of time, you've experienced the fatigue that can only be overcome by taking lots of breaks.

You also have interruptions. A 2008 study at UC Irvine measured the time cost of interruptions with office workers. (Note that 2008 was just the BEGINNING of the smartphone age, so you can imagine how much worse it is now.) Their findings were as follows:

- After a distraction, it takes 23 minutes and 15 seconds to get back into a flow state

- The average worker switches tasks every 3 minutes

- We SELF-interrupt ourselves the most, i.e. switching to Facebook or eBay when we should be doing something important

- This surprised me quite a bit: When we eliminate distractions, we work SLOWER because there's less urgency to complete a task before the next distraction

The last point taps into Parkinson's Law: work expands to fill the time allotted for its completion. This tells me we're screwed either way: we can either complete lots of little tasks (let's call them "pebbles" for fun), or a few larger tasks (or "rocks").

Think in terms of milestones, not percentage of progress. What are the four most important things you can do today, such that everything else is not important?

One of your tasks should be something easy. I teach everyone I know to plan to do one 10-minute task during the day, then a 40-minute task, another 40-minute task, and another 40-minute task, with breaks in-between.

You can delegate. You can batch up tasks if needed. You can meet with partners or workers to get tasks knocked out. But I'm telling you: regularly pulling all-nighters and marathon sessions is NOT sustainable. You'll burn out.

Investor Warren Buffet states, "You can't create a baby in 1 month by getting 9 women pregnant." If a recipe calls for you to bake a cake for 30 minutes at 350 degrees and you're short on time, baking for 15 minutes at 700 degrees will NOT give you the same result!

Suggestion #2: It's Easier to Edit Crap Than Air

In my own business, when I'm indecisive, I tell myself two things: first, that I must keep things shippable. Second, that I must allow my customers to vote with their wallets.

Software development has a term called the Minimum Viable Product. Ben Prater calls it "simpleware." Whatever project you're working on needs to get into the "done" state, even in raw, rough draft form, as soon as possible. Only then can you improve.

No offense, but the way you perceive the world in your imagination is extremely flawed. Have you ever thought about meeting up with a friend, and you thought to yourself what that conversation would be like? Who would say what, where the conversation would go? It never worked out that way, did it?

Many of us have some idea in our heads about that wonderful book we could write or that great presentation we could give, and we think we imagine it in vivid detail, but in reality, the gaps are not filled in. It's easy to envision the perfect website or the perfect article, but it's only that way because it's still stuck in your imagination. Not in the real world.

I once had a coaching client who was dead-set on teaching her system which explained how to quit your 9-to-5 day job in nine years. I asked her if there was a way to make it more exciting and fast-paced. If a 47-year-old mother with an 8-year-old son is tired of their daily grind, you're telling me this imaginary buyer has to wait until she's 56 and her son is 17 in order to retire? Who is asking for that problem to be solved? Is there a way to shortcut the process to 6 months or even 90 days?

If you'll allow me to be blunt, I believe many people (including myself) are insecure about their ideas, their business, their marketing and their training. A common trap is to attempt to overcome insecurity with complexity. Appearing ultra-smart and bragging about a system taking 9 years to complete or bragging about a training course containing 92 hours of videos. That sounds overwhelming to your prospect.

In college, I had a friend who struggled to write an essay. As I helped her to write some of it, I understood why: she'd write half a sentence, then delete the entire sentence. Half a sentence, then delete. After 10 attempts, finally, that one sentence was complete. It took the time and effort of ten sentences to write one!

That sounds like the most discouraging way of working to me. Instead, what about multiple passes? Write a sentence, even it's not the most cleverly worded turn-of-phrase, so you get the idea down on paper. Then, when you have time:

- Spend 10 minutes here and there making a quick pass. Perhaps spend one minute per page editing.

- Scan the document to see if any unnecessary words can be crossed out to tighten things up.

- Read your paragraphs backwards to see if any awkwardness is obvious, such as transitions.

- Rate the paragraphs in your document on a score of 1 to 10 and only edit those paragraphs with the lowest scores, i.e. turn all the 5's into 7's.

You may not be at all interested in writing or proofreading, but I hope you get the point. If improvisation and willpower are failing you, develop a strategy of attack to get it done.

It helps to be optimistically pessimistic. In other words, hope for the best and plan for the worst.

Suggestion #3: You Need to Get Started

Almost always, when I was stuck at some point in my life, the answer was to get started. Let's say you've always wanted to travel the world, but life got in the way. Why not take the smallest baby step to start? You'd take that baby step anyway.

Since we were just talking about writing and schoolwork, I'm sure you've been at a point in your life when you procrastinated writing an essay or finishing a project. Once you started, it was easy. Perhaps the solution was to spend 10 minutes on it. After writing a few sentences during those ten minutes, you found your groove and, suddenly, you spent an hour and were halfway done.

Let's apply this same logic to traveling the world. You don't have to backpack through Europe or visit the Great Wall of China. Book a weekend flight and hotel to Hawaii or New York City to give yourself a change of scenery. To simplify even further, it may help you to only do research and see which island in Hawaii you'd like to see, which flights would work for you, what activities you'd like to do there and what the cost will be so you can get a budget and begin saving. Make a few small decisions.

Have you wanted to go back to college to get your degree? Get a brochure, read about classes or search online to book a tour. Have a dream car? Rent it for a week on Turo or visit CarMax to decide on the year, make, model, color, and price. Trying to conceive a child with your spouse but it's not happening yet? Don't leave things to chance, book an appointment with a fertility specialist.

Many of us know a person or have been a person who is single and bitter, yet unwilling to take that first step to join a dating site such as eHarmony or Match. How about the all-to-common problem of losing weight? Consider the person who buys countless diet books, protein shakes and home gym equipment, when a walk around the block twice a day would be an easier start. Setup successful habits for yourself!

We're looking to avoid the classic self-fulfilling prophecy. There's no reason to try, I've already decided the outcome, and I feel good because I'm right. Would you rather be right or be happy?

Self-sabotage can be a scary thing. "I'm not happy with my dating life and yet I don't put myself out there." "I hate my job but I'm not pursuing any other career opportunities." "I'm always late, tired and stressed out, yet I'm not organized with my time management." "I'm tired and feel terrible, yet I practice a poor diet."

A key revelation came to me when I discovered the difference between motivation and discipline. Many people say they can't build their business, market themselves or do the needed work because they're not excited or motivated enough. The problem with motivation is it's extremely unreliable and it's tied to your emotions. If you wake up on the wrong side of the bed tomorrow morning and you're not inspired, does that mean you can't "work?"

Discipline. Set rules for yourself such as the hours you'll work, the actions you'll take, your commitments, deadlines, appointments, projects and tasks. Many times, you don't "feel like" taking action, but once you do, it becomes fun after you get that sense of accomplishment that comes from taking action.

In college, I had yet another friend who had good grades, a perfect 4.0 GPA, all A's. He seemed smart, but wasn't an over-the-top genius, nor a complete workaholic. His secret? He simply worked the hours of 9AM to 5PM on his schoolwork. Studying, writing, reading, performing tasks for a project, researching and visiting the professor during office hours. He avoided the stress of all-nighters and uncertainty.

One of my favorite stories is about a man named Michael Lotito. His claim to fame was that he ate nine tons of metal during his lifetime. Not only that, but he ate 18 bicycles, 15 shopping carts, a number of beds, TV's, a computer and even an entire airplane!

His secret? Michael ground up the metals into a fine powder and sprinkled a small amount on his food every day. How do you eat a bicycle or an elephant? One bite at a time.

Suggestion #4: Don't Get Caught Up in the Mechanics

We've established that you should commit to the handful of important tasks each day, get the rough cut (or rough draft) done so you can edit later and get started.

Question: how's your current sense of urgency? Whatever pressing task you have, are you prepared to take the proper action now instead of waiting for the stars to align? Most things can be revised later, and many times, any tool will do the job.

George R.R. Martin, writer of the "Game of Thrones" books, uses an MS-DOS computer from the mid-1980's to get his writing done. Would it make any difference if he used a top-of-the-line MacBook Pro? The computer on board the Space Shuttle (which ran until 2011) used computer processors from 1985 (the i386) because it got the job done and there was less room for error.

Your actions can almost always be revised later. Do me a favor: browse to one of your favorite YouTube channels, for example, Gary Vaynerchuk or Ray William Johnson. Try to find their earliest video, perhaps from 2007 or 2009. You'll notice they used a worse camera, had a worse haircut and had worse content and editing than the "refined" look you now see after thousands of hours of improvement. They had to start somewhere!

Don't let your analysis of what tool (camera, other equipment, software, course, mentor) to use hold you back from taking the dedicated, massive imperfect action you know you need to take (in your life and/or your business).

Recently, a friend posted a video in a private Facebook group that was successfully landing new clients. I immediately took note of the video's structure and talking points, and within an hour, recorded my own video modeled after his (which this person recommended I do). Afterwards, I noticed that most of the comments under his post were from people asking, "What camera did you use to film that?" The answer: ANY camera.

I was looking at content quality, not production quality. One of my favorite marketers, Russell Brunson, told a story over a decade ago that has stuck with me ever since. He was learning the guitar and bought a DVD from eBay. The video disc arrived in the mail, he inserted it into his player and pressed play. At first, the screen was completely black, although guitar sounds could be heard.

After a few seconds, a woman's voice sounded. The wife of the guitar instructor: "You forgot to take off the lens cap, honey!"

I was floored. It dawned on me on that day that good "production" quality is nice to have as long as it doesn't delay or get in the way of your "content" quality. If the choice is between a website, assignment, presentation, book or article that looks good but has bad content -- versus an "average" presentation with good content, I'll take ugly-but-useful every time.

Step #1: Ask the Right Questions & Write It Down. Secretary of Defense Donald Rumsfeld once made an interesting observation that any situation consists of known-knowns (things we know we know), known-unknowns (things we know we do not know), and unknown-unknowns (things we don't know we don't know).

Perhaps you're looking to create a website for your business, and you're simply overwhelmed with the possibilities. In the coming weeks, those unknown-unknowns will convert into known-unknowns, and your current task is to convert known-unknowns into known-knowns. A helpful exercise could be to list the questions you need answers to in order to take action. For example:

- What will I name my website?
- What will people see when they land on my website?
- What will my website address be?
- What platform will I use to host my website?

Once questions are listed, your subconscious automatically begins to answer them. (Pop quiz: what's 3 times 3?) Since you're also looking to build habits of consistent progress and completion, it may help to write in a journal every day. (Monday: "What are 20 possible names for my website?")

As a marketer, you're looking to convey information on a web page, blog post, webinar, podcast interview, live presentation, etc. The best starting point for any of those things are your own personal notes -- souped-up and turned into templates.

If you want to teach someone about payroll taxes, what existing notes (bullet points) could you refine into a polished presentation anyone could understand? If you're writing a book about retirement planning, what would YOU want to know? If you're interviewed about real estate, how would you teach it to a friend?

Step #2: Set a Deadline. You most likely have so many things going on in your life, that if something important is not on your calendar (with reminders), then it won't get done. You're chipping away at a large project you can't complete in one sitting, so you must revisit it regularly. However, avoid the trap of neglect -- letting progress go by the wayside for months at a time.

Commit to completing the assignment by a specific date AND time, i.e. by 5PM on the first of next month. To add fuel to the fire, tell someone you know (your spouse in person, a friend via email) about your intentions. Follow-up with that person after the due date to verify it was done. There's definitely a psychological aspect to telling someone else about your task and deadline, and using the fear of letting that person down as the "drive" to finish.

Step #3: Revisit, Iterate & Ramp-Up. Let's say you have a limited budget. Write and edit your own Kindle book. You film your YouTube channel using your iPhone. Get started in a simple fashion. After you experience success, improve as you make progress on the journey towards unconscious competence.

You may have heard the secret to success of even the most pro-level athletes is daily practice and repetition. Have you ever played a sport, even for fun? When I practiced Little League baseball from ages 8 to 10, the majority of our practice sessions involved catching fly-balls or grounders, again and again. The secret to good grades for many students out there is to create a study guide for a test, and then copy it again and again until it becomes automatic.

As you improve your marketing, websites, books and so on, invent your own technology: terms, phrases, sayings, acronyms or sound bites. Grant Cardone is a master at coining catchphrases which explain his concepts: Who's Got My Money, Be Obsessed Or Be Average, Success Is My Duty, Whatever It Takes, 10X. These aren't merely platitudes, but concepts made unique by these phrases.

One Stop Shop. Hustle. No Annual Contracts. Paleo Diet. There's An App For That. Information Superhighway. Y2K "Bug." Just Do It. Dumpster Fire. Fake News. Gaslighting. Subprime Mortgage. Financial Crisis. YOLO. FOMO. Some of these terms are dated, but they were at one point used so frequently that you instantly understood this secret language.

As you ramp-up, eliminate the unessential. Think back to when you first learned to drive a car. Everything was new. Mirrors, gas, brake, turn signal, other cars, current speed, cruise control, windshield wiper blades. Staying in your own lane, stop signs, yellow lights, yield signs, right of way, pedestrians. After a few months of driving, you abstracted away most of your surroundings into five or so attributes: speed limit, who's in front of or behind you, next turn, traffic light or stop sign, current lane. You could perform previously complex maneuvers like turn signals, U-turns, and pulling into parking spaces with almost zero thinking.

The same is true with the way you learned to tie your shoes, the speed at which you type on your phone's keyboard or the way you walk. Difficult at first, now automatic.

Step #4: It's All About the Template. Zig Ziglar says, "Repetition is the mother of learning." You only start from scratch that first awkward time. Usually, when I create a new website (using WordPress), I clone a site (or page), gut the contents, and rebuild. The same is true for PDF reports and books. Copy the previous project and edit.

Don't start from scratch. I use templates in my business and marketing. Webinar presentations, sales letters (respond to the same questions with new answers), cold prospecting emails, outsourcing.

Example: I run a podcast that's hosted hundreds of guests. You'll find out about some of them in upcoming chapters! Producing hundreds of episodes requires quite a bit of time and labor. I need to find new guests, record interviews with those guests, produce those recordings into episodes and promote.

- Finding guests: I write instructions detailing how to comb through some of my favorite podcast shows and build a spreadsheet of guest interviewees on those podcasts, including contact information. There's also a procedure to take that list and mail merge it into outgoing episodes to ask people to appear on my show. If they accept, they choose a timeslot using my online calendaring system.

- Interviewing guests: I do this myself, but we can abstract our interview into a series of reliable questions and answers to reduce thinking. I start with the person's bio, ask what they've been up to with online marketing in the last 30 days, what makes that person stand out, what a beginner can do to find initial success modeling them, and the low hanging fruit / do's-and-don'ts listeners can absorb if they're struggling. Along the way, I recap that person's answers to ensure I understand. To wrap up, I ask, "If people were impressed by our conversation and want to find out more about you, where should they go?" That guest provides a website address, known as a call-to-action.

- Producing podcast episodes: Without getting too technical, uploading a podcast episode involves adding an audio clip to state the title of that episode, music, and a commercial at the end. The audio file is compressed into an MP3, tagged, uploaded and added to a blog post with links and notes.

- Podcast promotion: Once the podcast episode is online, I'll promote via email, Facebook, Twitter and sometimes LinkedIn. Sometimes, I'll pay someone to take notes about the episode or create a written transcript.

I can perform the above steps myself for the first few episodes of my podcast to get it done quickly, then explain the steps I'm taking using a free screen capture tool called UseLoom. It has the effect of showing the exact clicks I perform on the computer, with my voice narrating it. (Imagine a person looking over my shoulder onto my computer screen, but in playable YouTube video form.) I can hire someone on an outsourcing site like Upwork to perform my exact instructions onto 10 or 20 podcast episodes at a time.

I'm hoping you realize your business and marketing efforts will never be perfect. What's more important is you act quickly, produce lots of different things, adjust and then scale. It doesn't matter if you have the fanciest and fastest computer with all the latest software. What matters is you use that computer to create a money-making website, app or consulting business.

Who cares if your website (or business, or career, in general) is pretty or ugly? Your key metrics -- traffic, conversion and cashflow -- are more important. Results beat perfection.

Next Steps

1. Can you reduce your daily tasks to just four per day?

2. Have you set deadlines to complete projects in a timely fashion?

3. Can you write down 2-5 questions to ensure you're solving the right problems?

Chapter 2: The Perfect Day Formula by Craig Ballantyne

Are you stressed out? Do you feel like you're running out of time, procrastinating or are unhappy? Craig Ballantyne is called the world's most disciplined man by his friends and his coaching clients, and he's the author of "The Perfect Day Formula: How to Own the Day and Control Your Life", and he's the creator of the world-famous fat burning workout system.

Here's what makes The Perfect Day Formula unique. Many time management books only tell you what to do during your work day. Instead, this new plan is a wholistic approach to make the most of your entire life. It's based on the 3C formula:

- Control your mornings
- Cope with the chaos of the world in the afternoon
- Concentrate on what counts at night

We put structure into our day so we can get work done and still get home in time for quality family, hobby, and friend time, which is important but missing from many peoples' lives.

Back in 2006 when I was a young 30-year-old man, I was successful with my online fitness business, Turbulence Training, with thousands of customers all over the world. It allowed me to quit my job as a personal trainer, but then I started working at all hours of the day, I celebrated all hours of the night. I suffered from anxiety attacks so bad I visited the emergency room twice over a six-week period. I said, "I think I'm having a heart attack." It was the lowest point of my life, and that's when I realized I needed more structure. I was waking up too late, which caused stress and anxiety. I made a deal with myself: I would wake up five minutes earlier the following day.

Over time, I repeated this five minute habit to incrementally "work my way back" into earlier wake-up times, until I felt comfortable. I was finally waking up at a time of day that was right for me. Please note, if this doesn't suit your personality, you don't have to get up early in the morning. It's not about the hour you get up, it's about what you do with the hours you are up.

Doing things early in the morning before distractions come about is one of the best ways to operate. That's what I learned back then, and I implemented a bunch of new systems over the years which allowed me to become a more productive person. In fact, some people call me the most productive person they know.

Many people think, "I don't want rules for my life. I already have rules from the government, my career, my boss, my industry." People get resistant when rules are imposed upon them by other people, but when we create rules for our own life, it sets us free.

Creating rules for your life is like having an effective operating system in your iPhone or MacBook, and this operating system within our electronics allows our electronics to do amazing things. We want to have our own personal operating systems for ourselves that reduce the amount of discipline we need and the amount of willpower that we require. Therefore, if we have this operating system and these rules in place for our life, we become more efficient. We don't have to make more decisions.

This happens in the real world. Steve Jobs wore the same turtleneck outfit every day and Mark Zuckerberg wears his gray t-shirt and hoodie. These successful people wear the same boring outfits because that "outfit choice" is one less decision to make in the morning. Rules for our life allow us to do these things. If you have a rule that you go to bed at eleven o'clock every night during the week, you're won't be tempted to stay up until one o'clock in the morning watching some playoff game. You'll say, "I go to bed at eleven o'clock every night, that's my rule. I'm not breaking the rule because people know about it, and I don't want to go in tired tomorrow and have people say, "What did you do? Did you lie and break your rule?" No. We want to always operate within our rules. I help people develop five or six rules for their life.

Rule #1: Choose what time you go to bed and what time you wake up. Go to bed at the same time and wake up at the same time every day. That gives you all-day energy. It sounds boring, and you might break that rule once or twice a week because you'll stay awake for social activity. That's fine, but don't sleep in. That throws you off track. Set your bedtime and wake-up time.

Rule #2: First thing in the morning, work on your number one priority for fifteen minutes. That number one priority can be a problem you're trying to overcome, like getting out of credit card debt, or it can be an opportunity you're trying to take advantage of, which may be a marketing plan, or maybe a health plan, or maybe even time with spiritual work if you want to improve your relationship with God. That's your number one priority in life. Get up and focus fifteen minutes on it first thing in the morning.

You don't have to wake up at five o'clock in the morning, I'm not telling you to take drastic action and wake up three hours earlier. What I'm saying is just get up and spend fifteen minutes of clear, uninterrupted thinking on your number one priority. If you're trying to write a book, you can write 500 words in fifteen minutes. In ten weeks, that's a 30,000-word mini-book. That shows you can make amazing progress in fifteen minutes at a time. That's the second rule. Make sure you spend fifteen minutes working on your number one priority.

Rule #3: Follow one foundational health rule every day. Take care of your health. You can't be burning the candle at both ends, so it might be related to meditation, an exercise program, or the diet you follow. Choose one health rule that gives the biggest bang for your buck and has the biggest impact on your life. Don't think, "I need to do 900 things for my health." Do the one major thing that make the biggest impact.

Rule #4: Spend some time on your number one wealth building activity every day. If it's podcasts, record a podcast every day. If it's writing a book, write 1,000 words a day. If it's a sales presentation, do at least one sales presentation and practice your sales presentation for a half an hour a day. Whatever it is that builds wealth, do it every day.

Rule #5: Your not-to-do rule. What's one thing you should not do because it interrupts your progress at night? It might be drinking alcohol during the week, checking email before 8AM, or arguing with work colleagues. Tell yourself, "I won't do this because it holds me back in life." Say, "This is my new not-to-do rule." When those five rules are in place, you don't need many others. Begin with those. It makes you an effective operating machine.

Have that not-to-do rule because we can do several things correctly, but bad habits eliminate our good habits. Here's an extreme example that gets the point across: you have a recovering alcoholic who drinks water, says the serenity prayer and goes to his meetings six and a half days a week, then on Friday afternoon goes to a bar, that can wipe out all the good stuff he's done in the past week. It's because he's breaking that one not-to-do rule.

We're all human and have negative things in our life. For me, it was email. For the longest time, I had to fight it so hard because it would get me down a rabbit hole. I would see one negative email, and thinking about a snappy comeback for the entire morning would stop me from writing my book. That's when I realized humans need to have a not-to-do rule to protect themselves from distractions and temptations.

"Rules" came from my weight loss transformation clients. I ran before-and-after weight loss contests for many years. Those who won had rules about nutrition, what they ate, and how they said no when attending a birthday party. They stuck to rules. Everyone needs rules for their lives.

A public accountability partner is best. Tell your friends and the world, via your Facebook page, "These are my operating rules." When you tell people that, you don't want to be a hypocrite. That's one of the lowest forms of humanity, because people don't like to be seen as the type of person who says one thing but acts in a different way. Being a hypocrite is easy for people to give you a hard time about. That's how you stick to those rules.

Do we need to become a robot and never, ever break these rules? No, they're rules, not laws. Rules are meant to be broken, with discretion, from time to time, but laws are meant to be followed. Our rules can be broken, but we need to do it with discretion, and do it very infrequently.

Scenario: You say, "I won't drink during the week." You stick to that for nine months. You're a Chicago Cubs fan, and they win the World Series for the first time in 105 years. You'll have a drink because it's a Thursday night. You're celebrating with your father who never thought the Cubs would win a World Series. You can break that rule in circumstances like that, but you can't break the rule for something insignificant such as, "Tuesday night is bowling, that means I'll drink." No, you can't break the rule in that situation. It must be broken only in important circumstances.

Know yourself. If you can have potato chips in the house, and you have enough self-control to eat a handful of potato chips but not the entire bag, have potato chips on-hand and you can break that rule on occasion. However, if you're the type of person who "can't eat just one" and devours the entire bag, you'll search for those potato chips every night. In that case, set a rule not to store potato chips in the house. It makes it easier for you to stick to your goals.

There's space in between you wanting chips, and traveling to the grocery store to purchase them. This allows you self-control. Know yourself. Can I have cookies in the house? Can I have alcohol in the house? Can I have my phone beside my bed in the morning or will I check my email when I wake up?

Put these systems (or fences) in place, protect yourself from your bad habits. It's okay to go to extremes in some cases, especially when kicking a bad habit at the start, because that's when it's hardest to kick it. If you had a bad habit in the past, you've overcome it and you know you can enjoy it once in a while without going completely off the rails, then break that rule once in a while. But if you think, "This is the beginning of a four-month bender eating cookies constantly..." Keep yourself out of that trouble.

I'm the least disciplined and laziest person in the world, which is why these systems are in place. For example, I have an apartment in Denver (near our office) and a home in Toronto. In Denver, I don't have internet access at home, because if that was available, I'd be tempted to use it. I work at home for two hours without internet and get a lot done. I avoid sliding into old bad habits. I fight these things all the time, and when things do go wrong, I center myself to get back on track quickly. I don't feel bad or don't worry, and I don't say, "This day is entirely wasted, so I'll waste the rest of it." Forgive yourself. You can't change the past. You can only control your thoughts, words and deeds. Continue to make the right decisions for your right life.

To get the life you desire, start with vision. Know where you want your life to be: your career, where to live, and family. Where do you want your life to be in three to five years?

Close your eyes and watch the movie of your life. Write the movie script for your life as if you've already accomplished your big goals and dreams. You live in that dream house you've always wanted to live in. You're with your family. Your kids are fully grown. Describe your career, work hours, your family's habits and your own healthy habits. What do you do on the weekend? What do you do after work and after school? What do your annual family vacations and rituals look like? Get a clear picture of what your life will look like in three to five years.

If that's what you want life to look like, you can plan the steps to make it happen.

If you want to go to Disney World and you don't live in Orlando, fly to Orlando to go on this dream destination vacation. When you get there, rent a car, punch in the address into the GPS and drive to Disney World. You know exactly how to get to Disney World.

This vision for your life is your own personal Disney World. If you know where you want to go and what your goals are, determine the exact steps to take to get there. That simplifies life. This allows you to say "no" to many detours that get you off track and hold you back.

Goal setting is essential to getting what you want from life. There are good goals and bad goals. You need a vision in place first, and THEN set goals to get there. Most people set too many goals. They have 30 goals for this year, and that's too many. That's a shotgun scattered approach. We want a laser focused approach of a few goals. It's not setting an outcome goal such as, "I want to lose ten pounds in twelve weeks." That's a bad goal. You don't control it. You can do all the right things to get you there, but you can't control whether you lose exactly ten pounds. Focus on what you can control by setting process goals.

If I want to lose ten pounds in twelve weeks, my process goals that I can control are action steps. For instance, "I'll exercise three times per week. I'll follow this diet 90% of the time, and I'll drink three liters of water every single day." If I follow these three process goals, I'll get very close to my outcome goal.

Similarly, if I want to make an extra $10,000 a year, what do I need to do? One extra sales call a week? I can control that. I can't control the outcome of how much money I make, but I can control making that extra sales call.

I can control: spending an extra 30 minutes on my sales presentation or 30 minutes per week of practice time. I can control: having someone critique my sales presentation. I'll perform a sales presentation in front of a friend and ask, "Can you give me some feedback?" I can control those things. If I do those three things, they'll make me a better salesperson, give me a greater chance of making more money, and a greater opportunity of hitting that $10,000 outcome goal.

Start with the outcome goal in mind, and then set three process goals for it. Whether you want to lose weight or make more money, that is the outcome. Be specific, give yourself a timeframe, give yourself those process goals and make sure they fit into your daily perfect day, which you learn about in my book, *The Perfect Day Formula*.

Another key component to being successful is having a coach. The biggest mistake I made in my career was not hiring a coach early on. I didn't hire a coach until 2006, which was a pivotal year for me. I could have afforded a coach in 2003, so I waited three years too long. As soon as I hired my coach, I made more money. Go to a mastermind group and hire someone as a phone coach. If you can't afford that, buy their books, watch their videos and buy their courses until you can afford to go to their events. Every successful person needs a coach. Top pro athletes and CEO's say repeatedly, "There's someone out there better than me."

To get a free copy of my life's work shipped to you, pay shipping and handling at FreePerfectDayBook.com. Implement it just as the 12,000 other people who have bought it and used it in their life.

Next Steps

1. Have you decided what time you'll go to bed and what time you'll wake up?

2. Tomorrow morning, will you commit to working on your number one priority for 15 minutes? What is it?

3. What one foundational health rule will you begin to follow daily from now on? (i.e. meditation, exercise, diet)

4. What one wealth building activity will you pursue every day?

5. What one thing will you NOT do because it interrupts your progress at night? (i.e. drinking at night or checking email before 8AM)

Craig's Contact Information

- Instagram: @RealCraigBallantyne

- EarlyToRise.com (daily essays on success, making money and being more productive)

- FreePerfectDayBook.com (free copy of his best-selling book)

Chapter 3: Search Engine Optimization, Content Marketing, Pinterest and YouTube by Kellen Kautzman

Kellen Kautzman owns Send It Rising Internet Marketing at SendItRising.com. He manages a team of over 20 internet marketing professionals. Kellen was the keynote speaker at Planet

Hollywood on the Las Vegas Strip. His book, Everybody's Doing It, was the number one new release on Amazon.com in the SEO, search engine optimization, category. If you're looking to figure out how to improve your business and get better search results, you're in the right place.

When it comes to getting traffic to your website, Pinterest is a neglected piece of the puzzle. Through Google Search Console, also called Google Webmaster Tools, we can measure links. Pinterest goes viral quickly. If you're a small business owner and I bring up the word "Pinterest" to you, typically, the first response is, "What are you talking about? Pinterest? That won't do anything for me." Even if they're a florist, or some other person offering a service.

Pinterest works in any industry. Think of an electrician. If there is an infographic showing which wires are dangerous and which are less dangerous, or the color-coding of wires, someone somewhere is looking for that information... We had a dog rescue that created a "pin." It's a picture of a corgi. A tiny burrito-looking dog with legs.

The corgi has one paw up on a stair, and it says, "Life is short, and so are my legs." That was re-pinned 14,100 times. Because the image itself is a link back to the website, you can get exponential link building. We had a decorative rock landscaping company client, Parsons Rocks in Las Vegas, with one of the most mundane pictures of a backyard. For some reason, it took off on Pinterest, ended up with 3,000 re-pins, which means 3,000 links. Those links raise Google rankings, and you get paid. Do not neglect Pinterest as a link-building mechanism.

In Google Search Console, I've never seen a single link from Facebook. I've seen one link from Twitter. Google doesn't index these sites.

Is Pinterest destined to be the next Facebook or Twitter? I'm not sure Google indexes Pinterest and not Facebook or Twitter.

Facebook is a direct competitor, so that makes sense. Spam is prevalent on Twitter.

If they'll do it eventually, that's all the more reason to do it now. I didn't know what Pinterest was until a few years ago. People share arts and crafts, decorating ideas, food recipes, things us guys stereotypically don't care much about. Once I started looking at it closer, I realized it was a great way to build an idea bank.

How do we make this interesting in marketing terms? Regarding the viral image side, I take the perspective that education is key. If all else fails, just give them the information. If you're a plumber, tell internet visitors (prospective clients) how to fix their sink disposal, or unclog a drain. Let me add another social media platform, YouTube. You've uploaded a YouTube video and gone to the captions section. What you'll find in the upper-right-hand corner when you click on it, is YouTube has a 98% to 99% understanding of the words you're saying. The algorithm they're using is exceptionally good.

This tells us that content in the form of a blog is almost identical to content in the form of a video. They're both translated into the written word. If you're a small business owner and you can get out in front of your van with your company's advertising -- if you're an insurance agent, for example -- set up a camera and start talking. It will be ugly at first, and that's okay. My first videos were embarrassingly bad. That's part of the journey. Now we a $2500 camera equipment, tripod, wireless lapel mic and lighting. You don't start there. In fact, some of the videos that do the best are those that are a little grainy, as long as the content is good.

Google's artificial intelligence, married to YouTube, understands the words that come out of your mouth. When you think about content development, don't think, "I need my fingers to go numb from blogging so much," or, "I need to hire a company to blog on my behalf." That's good. That's fine. It's not going anywhere. Many small business owners are reluctant to overcome this junior high fear that we all tend to have, wherein we perspire if the camera is pointed in our general direction. I have clients who think they can knock out these videos, and the second the camera starts rolling, they melt down. They don't realize how hard it is to be on camera.

If you are making YouTube videos, I check out YouTube in-stream ads. We're getting cost-per-view at three cents, which is insane. One in eight of those people watch to 30 seconds, which is when you're charged those three cents. If you want a ton of impressions, you can target by city. We're doing Las Vegas. We're getting approximately 15,000 impressions, 3,000 views, for $100. It's hard to beat that.

If you become a small business owner, you now own a channel. Typically, the channels people own nowadays are extremely poor quality. By poor quality, for example, you have a YouTube channel on which the last video was three years ago. That could have been a great video, but it doesn't count if there's no consistency there. Raise the bar on the educational/entertainment value of what you're putting out there.

Consider something as mundane as a light bulb manufacturer. You could talk about energy production in the United States and how it relates to light bulbs. You could talk about how light bulbs are evolving, how smart homes are evolving with different technologies, and what those look like. You could talk about the stock price of the light bulb industry, how it's been great over the decades, and how it's a good investment. You could extend it all the way into art and these crazy different light bulbs people create. At the end of the day, every word we say is understood and measured by RankBrain, which is Google's artificial intelligence algorithm.

I used to think that AI was a programmer tweaking the code of a system that would do X, Y, or Z, based on what the programmer said. What's really happening with AI is that the programmers give the artificial intelligence a goal and walk away. As an example, there's this great Atari game, BreakOut. You hit a ball, and you're trying to break bricks. Once you break all the bricks at the top of the screen, you win.

Google taught their DeepMind AI to learn BreakOut. They said, "Get the maximum number of points." What's fascinating to me about the artificial intelligence is that it takes 60 minutes before it starts to learn a couple things. Another 60 minutes go by, and it learns some more things. Two or three days into it and it's mastered the game. One more piece of this puzzle is that English can be seen as a very complicated form of the game BreakOut. Google's understanding of the English language is incredibly good now.

Operate under the assumption there's a judge out there. Imagine you're in a courtroom and the judge is looking at all the mentions in your channels, everything you say and rendering a verdict. The verdict determines where you rank in Google search results.

Google is now so advanced with their artificial intelligence and their ranking that it doesn't pay to try to trick the system. If you do what's educational or entertaining and gives people what they want, Google's huge brain will figure it all out.

It's having a conversation with someone who's exponentially smarter than you. It's important to understand you have this intrinsic ability to advertise, that's number one. The word "advertising" comes from the Latin word "advertere" meaning "to turn toward." Anything you do as a business owner that gets somebody's attention is advertising. If you're on a podcast, running a Facebook ad, or if you're liking a post on Facebook, these are all examples of advertising.

It's a therapy session. If you don't value your own expertise, you're missing the point. If you don't think your industry is sexy or interesting, you're missing the point. What you do on a daily basis, for 99% of humanity, is outside their norm. It's more interesting than you think, and you're smarter and better at it than you think.

Teenagers are putting everything online. If you want to measure your ability to advertise, measure it against a 16-year-old, because people in your generation, whether you're an old millennial or baby boomer, you're only fighting against those in your same generation. If you're feeling anxious about making YouTube videos, feeling weird about tweeting as often as you think you should or embracing Snapchat or Pinterest, know that everyone else in your generation feels the same way. It's to your advantage to push forward.

I like the idea of making the YouTube videos, and running in-stream ads on other people's YouTube videos, especially if you're a plumber, for example. Run an ad for anyone searching for specific plumbing problems and set it to a certain radius.

Another example: magnesium campfire sticks are a fascinating e-commerce product that lends itself to tons of content ideas. If a

YouTube video had been created three years ago about campfire sticks, it would be an asset at this point. It's similar to real estate. There are moments where it dips, but generally, over the years, there is a steady increase in the asset's value.

Your average internet user understands that a website has a certain intrinsic value that grows over time. The same is true of any web asset, including a YouTube video. There could be a video with 20,000 views about setting up camping equipment in the Arctic. The feeling of having missed the opportunity will always be there. The opportunity, ironically, is always now. Now is always the best time to start. Now has all the best opportunities. You're missing out if you're not thinking about what you can do now.

Allow me to introduce you to a part of the mind called the *basal ganglia*. It's a walnut-shaped piece of your brain, towards the center which starts firing when you are on cruise control. Once something has been habituated, the basal ganglia will take over. There's a gentleman whose hippocampus was destroyed by a virus. His short-term memory was shot. He'd introduce himself to you repeatedly. They put a board in front of him where he was asked to choose X or Y, but he didn't know why he was choosing these things. One board had a red splotch which represented "bad" and a green splotch which represented "good."

Over the next few months, he chose the green option. When asked, "Why are you choosing the green and not red?" He said, "I don't know. I can't explain it to you. It feels right." This relates to what we're talking about because you should create a weekly YouTube video. The creative process is your own. Figure out exactly what it is that you want to talk about. If you force yourself to create a habit where, come hell or high water, you are creating a YouTube video every week, you'll end up with an amazing web asset, that, over time, will not only rank better in Google, but get a ton of views via YouTube. Who knows what will happen in 10 to 20 years? Video won't go anywhere.

I attended a charity event recently, hosted by Kim MacQuarrie, a four-time Emmy Award-winning documentary filmmaker. I had no idea how successful he was when I went to Cunningham Elementary School for his nonprofit event, Green Our Planet. Green Our Planet is a phenomenally interesting nonprofit specializing in raising money online to plant gardens in low-income schools. Kids plant the seeds, which involves the math and science curriculum. They harvest the fruits and vegetables and sell them at a farmer's market. There is both a business and economics curriculum attached to it. As a former teacher, I find this concept fascinating.

At this charity event, I did not have my nice camera and it was drizzling outside. I pointed the camera towards my face and started talking. That video has about 5,000 views now. That's one good example. Point your camera phone at your face and start talking. Feel free to go into a video production software afterwards, similar to iMovie. If you're on Mac, that's an easy one. There's also something called picture-in-picture that will apply to any video software that you use and allows you to create a news anchor square next to your head. Add whatever you want. It is possible to take some shaky, grainy footage and still turn it into a little higher production quality. The standard video I make is simply a head shot of me talking. I don't have time to spend making a video. I set up the camera and talk about my subject. I've been reading my new book *Everybody's Doing It* on YouTube. That's an easy video to make, because I'm reading from the book.

Record your screen using QuickTime. On PC, use Camtasia or Screencast-O-Matic.com. The first time you make a video, you'll mistakenly want it to be perfect. The irony is, a year from now, your worst video will be better than the best video you could create now. It's scary to think you'll put yourself out there and it won't be a good look. There is such a thing as being vulnerable and having people make fun of you, or end up with a product you're not proud of. It's tough. It's a deep reflection on how we feel about ourselves.

Reflect on the fact that this is what you do. This is your profession. If not you, then who? Don't be afraid to be goofy or silly. I did a video in Spanish where I had a beard for a while and then cut all of it except for a mustache and a little soul patch. I had a blast doing it. A few people made fun of me, but I'm okay with that. Putting yourself out there will literally make you sweat. You pushed forward in an arena that people can't navigate.

Be bold. Be courageous. Be yourself. Be funny. Be serious. Do your thing. You can do this and create a habit out of it.

I have a master's degree in education, and I taught for five years prior to transitioning into the world of internet marketing. I find it interesting there's a ton of crossover between almost everything I look at. I mentioned "advertere", which is the Latin root of the word "advertising," means "to turn toward." We all had a very similar experience when we landed on this planet. The first thing we did was cry. That single act met our needs. It was our first advertisement.

As we grow to two, three and four years old, that simple advertisement turns into more subtle things, like holding out your hands if you want to be held, or going to the refrigerator if you're hungry. Develop language, "Like it," "Please," those sorts of things. We continue advertising throughout our entire lives. In fact, it's impossible not to. This notion that you aren't an amazing advertiser isn't true. Advertising is an innate human quality.

When we look at things that seem complicated, challenging and difficult, like Facebook demographic targeting, advanced Google Ads, Google Analytics and developing a WordPress website, what you'll find as you approach these spaces is you know this. It's intuitive. You know what you want to share with people, what looks and sounds good. The rest is figuring out the tools. In *Everybody's Doing It*, we show you that, but within the context of the fact you are already an excellent advertiser.

Everybody's Doing It covers SEO, Facebook, YouTube, Google Ads, Pinterest and link building advertising. I've had the small business owner conversation 2,000+ times. I know what the original conversation looks like and this book is 137 pages of me saying what I wish I could say in those meetings. If you're interested in my conceptual best practices of small business advertising, this is it.

If you want to take your business to the next level reach out to my team and we'll and make it happen.

Next Steps

1. Do you have a Pinterest account to watch out for viral images you can use to promote your business?

2. Will you record and post a YouTube video within the next 30 days?

3. Will you run a YouTube in-stream ad to increase your traffic?

Kellen's Contact Information

- **Amazon:** Everybody's Doing It: Advertising Redefined by SEO Expert Kellen Kautzman

- SendItRising.com: internet marketing agency for SEO, social media, and PPC

- KellenKautzman.com (official site)

Want to Tell Us What You Think About This Book So Far?

Email: robert@robertplank.com

All incoming emails will be read.

Chapter 4: Transition to the Next Stage of Your Life by Terri Rose

Terri Rose is a love and lifestyle coach. She's a motivational speaker committed to serving those in major life transitions, such as separation, divorce, single parenting, empty-nesting and/or losing a job. Terri encompasses the qualities of love and service to others.

The magic I provide is supporting people through difficult transitions with love and encouragement to help them overcome challenges, which makes them question their ability to make it through.

My specialty involves helping people go through the transitions of separation and divorce, empty nesting and single parenting. There's support out there for financial and legal advice in those areas, but as far as being helped emotionally and supported through those experiences, there aren't many avenues to support that need.

Family and friends serve in providing some emotional support, but it's difficult for them to stay unbiased. They have their own life circumstances. They aren't totally available in the way you need them when you're moving through rough life transitions.

That's where I come in. I've gone through that experience myself personally through a divorce. I realized, had I had somebody like me earlier on in that process, it probably would have closed the gap for me on some of the emotional suffering I went through during that process. I will coach you, keep you uplifted and encourage you. There is a light at the end of the tunnel. That's what I'm here to provide for people.

Most of my clients are moving through recent separations or divorces. I host a local Meetup group in my community, and that seems to be the predominant place where people come forth and need support. That's where I give most of my energy.

Some attendees of the Meetup group are in the raw grief state and others have journeyed through a couple years of the process and they're starting to get their feet back on the ground. Some people "in-between" are struggling with guilt for leaving their spouse.

Some struggle with feelings of failure and loss, and are internally processing what may have gone wrong. Everyone is in a different stage of those "five stages of divorce"... grief, anger, bargaining, depression and acceptance.

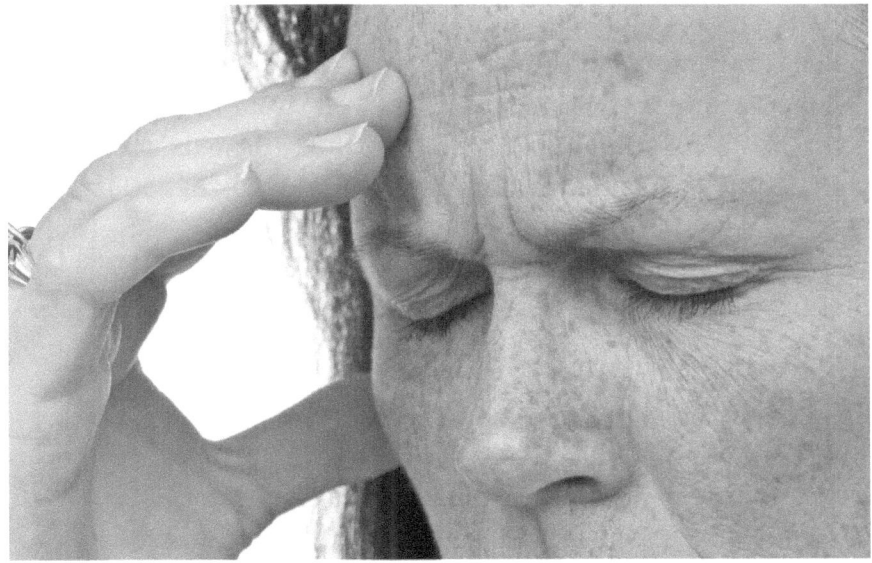

For the most part, my clients come to me in that stage of grief, denial, anger, or bargaining. They haven't shifted into the acceptance stage yet. I'm getting the ones that are earlier on in the process, which is great for me, because I've experienced it firsthand. I can give you hope, encouragement, and the empowerment to move forward slowly.

If you're struggling emotionally, implement self-care. Women don't do a good job at this because we raise families. We're the caretakers, we run the households and manage the kids. Many single parent dads do the same thing. We forget to take care of ourselves. We're depleted.

Set aside 15 minutes a day for yourself to read, walk, exercise, talk to a friend, or take a bath. Go swimming or laugh. Take 15 minutes a day and create that discipline, because it helps balance everything you're feeling and moving through emotionally. It carves out a better space for you to manage it.

When going through the divorce process, dealing with separation and the loss of family, some days, you won't want to get out of bed. There's not always going to be somebody there to show up at your door to pick you up and say, "Let's have a cup of coffee," or, "Let's go for a walk." You must be able to do that for yourself. If you don't, it's a downward spiral and it can suck you into the depth of despair, which is the place I'm committed to helping people not stay in.

Sometimes you need a day or two to feel grief and emotions, but you must shift out. Sometimes when you're in it, you can't do it alone. Somebody like me as your coach can come in and be there to mentor you, encourage you and give you different little exercises that help you stay focused on moving forward.

I'm a nature lover and outdoor gal and one of the pictures you'll see on my website reflects this. Put your hands into a Y-shape up to the sun, feel the sun on your face and stand rooted and grounded in that position, allowing the flow of sunlight, to feel those rays on your body and be present for a few seconds. To do that is an exercise that can shift you positively in big ways.

I'm a proponent of having one-person dance parties. Find a song that resonates, that makes your soul feel some joy and dance with yourself. I'm also a proponent of sticky notes of positive energy and positive vibe messaging keep you moving in a positive way. Gratitude journals are always good. Staying focused on gratitude and positive thinking is another way. You can take a hike or go for a walk in nature. I'm a strong proponent of water. Water helps me feel more grounded and lighter. For those that resonates with, water's always a great way to lighten up, relax and breathe.

Through this process, be tender with yourself. Have a good coach by your side encouraging you along the way and reminding you you're not alone.

An exercise I assign to my clients: write down three things you're grateful for. When you stay focused on gratitude, it's difficult to stay in anger, resentment, bitterness, hurt, pain, loss and grief. I help them focus on seeing their ex-spouse in some positive way so the energy doesn't stay focused on the fight, loss and negativity.

I have sticky notes that say, "My life moves forward through desire." "I am growing and changing with each new day." Do different things that resonate with the individual, something as simple as, "I am beautiful." "I am amazing." "I am lovable." Many of my clients struggle with that. I will never forget when I left my marriage of 13 years, one of the last things my ex-husband had said at the time was, "You'll never find somebody who loves you as much as I love you." I took that to heart and had to spend years accepting that I'm going to be lovable again. Simple mantras work wonders.

My ex-husband and I were great at being roommates and logistical partners. We had children but didn't have local family support to watch our children. During that time, his profession was aspiring, and I always wanted to be a stay-at-home mom. As his profession grew, I realized my dream. He worked hard to provide that opportunity for us as a family, which I will forever remain grateful for. However, he was away for a while. I felt alone and single raising the kids. When he was home, there was so much to do to keep up with the house, yard and cars. We grew apart but did well as logistical roommate partners running a family.

Not having family support to watch our children so we could get away as husband and wife took its toll on us over time and we grew apart. When you don't have the skills to be able to bring it back together and one or the other isn't able, willing or capable to get into the ring and fight for it, there's not a whole lot you can do.

It took that path. For myself, I realized it was time for me to leave that situation That's not how I wanted my children to learn what a marriage between a man and a woman was like. We did our best, but it's something I couldn't stay in anymore, so I chose to leave after a 13-year marriage.

I always say, "It's always about timing and alignment and things in our life." Particularly coming to a decision to end a marriage and break up a family is definitely not one that's made overnight. It's something that happens over a long period of time. In my case, it was a couple years of feeling unhappy, and I believe he was unhappy. We were going through it without communicating.

It came down to a moment for me when I had been tired of crying myself to sleep at night and feeling lonely in a marriage. That is another emotional prison that is not a healthy place to stay. One morning in the shower, I heard God whisper to me, "Trust, believe in the possibilities and don't be afraid. Don't think that I'm moving you away from something. I'm moving you towards something." It was in that moment, literally, with the water running over me and hearing those words, that gave me the courage to finally say, "I can't stay with it this way anymore."

The timing and alignment was off. When he was willing to fight, I was despondent. When I was ready to fight, he had checked out. Eventually everything aligned up where we agreed, "Let's end it."

It's never an easy choice and it's not a simple process, for sure. The way I best equate it is like when we talk about the loss and the grief that you go through, those same stages in divorce that you do when you lose a loved one. There's one key difference, which is you know when you lose someone you love you're not going to see them anymore, where in this case you continue to see them, interact with them and communicate with them if you have children. That makes it even more painful and doubly difficult to learn how to create a new normal way of living with loss, because they're there. You see them at kids' activities. You're communicating and coordinating logistics.

If you're not healthy in the beginning stages and being amicable with them, the one you end up hurting the most are those children. Revenge, anger, resentment and all those kinds of emotions that can rise up when we're hurt and the grief can be very, very damaging. In the end, as adults, we have the emotional maturity to move on and work through that. In the end, the children suffer.

The thing that helped me the most was repeating to myself, "Forgive him, for he knows not what he does. He's hurt," because it hurt him when I left. When one chooses to leave the relationship, that does hurt. That is what helped me through the hard times and the difficult painful times I experienced. I kept looking with forgiveness and understanding that, he's hurt. He's trying to hurt me because he's hurt.

It allowed me to stay in that higher vibrational level of love, gratitude, thankfulness and appreciation for him, as hard as it was.

Getting through the pain to the point of being okay is different for everyone. I am a woman built not to break. If you try to break me, I'll show you that you're won't succeed. I have quite a tenacious attitude and resilience within myself. My greatest challenge was faced with not only the divorce itself, but we had been living together in our home for six months when we decided to divorce. It took a judge to court order one of us out of the house. Believe it or not, most would say, "A judge would not take a stay-at-home mom with little ones out of the home." I was the one ordered to leave.

Pressure was on me at the beginning when I had to leave. I had to find a place to live and, because I had been a stay-at-home mom for 11 years, I had to reenter the workforce, which was a real challenge. I had exited the workforce before the Internet, and I had to enter the workforce with this new thing called the Internet. I had lost 11 years of experience to compete with my counterparts, so that created another challenge reentering the workforce. Many "whammies" hit me all at once.

It takes about two years to feel like you're "coming out of it" and stable. During that period, people date and participate in social activities to avoid rejection, loss and hurt. I tell my clients that it's okay to do that. Naturally, we're human and we need companionship. At the end of the day, you're not emotionally available for two years.

Life throws you curve balls. Decide how you'll meet it at the plate. Do you choose to let the ball hit you, knock you down and keep you down, or do you get up and run? I choose to get up and run. I've been laid off three times in seven years, so I restart all the time.

Take a step back. The universe could be trying to get your attention, move you to something different and show you something about yourself. The lessons can be quite insightful, if you're open to that.

When these changes come to us, they're there to move us in some positive way. It's how we choose to look at it based on our life experiences. If we choose to see it as negative and think, "Why does this always happen to me?" You'll keep attracting these things that keep happening to you. If you meet it with a positive attitude of, "Okay, I guess I wasn't meant to stay in that job," that means when that door closed, a new door of opportunity is opening up to you. I can't wait to see what it's going to be next. With that energy, you'll start attracting new opportunities. It always comes down to timing, alignment and our mindset.

Our belief systems have been built from experiences in the families we've been raised in, but as adults, we get the choice. We get to choose if we want to stay in that pattern and decide whether it has been working for you or not. You get to choose every day in every moment how you want to respond and allow it to either give you power or take away your power.

I'm committed to coaching people to their personal power and to always choose to take that positive step.

For more information, go to BlissifyYourLife.com, or email me at love@blissifyyourlife.com. I can also be reached via phone at 916-425-8383.

I offer a free 30-minute personal coaching session that's available to anyone who wants to talk and get to know me more. Talk to me on a personal, intimate level. I'm more than willing to share. I am here to love, serve and create a moment to empower people for greater strength and to thrive in their lives and design a life they love living, rather than live with the feeling of surviving.

I'm an old-school girl. I want to reach out, look you in the eye, touch, and hug you. I'll let you know it will be okay. I am the gal to personally connect with.

I also host a Meetup group once a month. It's a divorce support group all about saying YES to yourself. "YES" stands for "Your Empowered Self" through the process of divorce. It meets in Roseville, California, usually the last Friday night of each month. I hold them at the Holistic Lighthouse in downtown Roseville. Finding Your Empowered Self Through the Divorce Process.

People are typically glad to be a part of the group. Surprisingly, more men than women attend, which I love, because I feel the world needs more of a male voice in emotional pain and challenges. The women and men who have come have been very open and very revealing. They have all given me feedback stating I create a very safe space for them which feels comfortable for them to trust and open up, because their hearts are hurting. I bring together people who are going through the same type of process. It makes them feel safe.

Don't hesitate to come. I urge you to come and check it out. You'll make friends along the way who can relate to what you're feeling and experiencing.

There's that Roseville Meetup and blissifyyourlife.com, love@blissifyyourlife.com, 916-425-8383 to give me a call, chat with me and tell me what your situation is. I will be able to help you to get from point A to point B, help you to get to where you need to go. Don't devolve into bad, negative thinking, childish, immature, hurtful behavior. Because who does that help?

Next Steps

1. Do you implement self-care? If not, what self-care can you commit to for 15 minutes per day, i.e. exercise, bath, etc.?

2. Do you have a coach or mentor?

3. What three things are you grateful for?

4. Have you written down your three gratitudes on post-it notes and placed them in easy view?

5. Is there any negative self talk in your thought process? What can you eliminate?

Terri's Contact Information

- Website: BlissifyYourLife.com
- Email: love@blissifyyourlife.com
- Phone: 916-425-8383

Check out other episodes of our podcast with amazing guests:

MarketerOfTheDay.com

Listen and subscribe!

Chapter 5: Parse Your Story to Meet Your Audience by Jeanne Alford

Do you want to get your message out there and spark attention? Author, speaker, and communications expert, Jeanne Alford is the person to help you do it. Jeanne has directed PR and communications programs for Dolby Laboratories, Phillips Electronics, Visa, and Sony. She focuses on media perception, crisis communications and international issues.

As an executive coach, Jeanne specializes in communications and media training including speaking, presenting, and writing to guide business leaders to tell their most compelling stories in their own words.

Some people suffer from a syndrome I like to refer to as the shoemaker's daughter. We all think the same thing about ourselves. What we do is ordinary, because we're in it every day. We don't always see the extraordinary, so sometimes you do need a third party, somebody outside with expertise to come in and say, "Let's talk about it."

When we communicate, we exchange information. If we don't understand our audience and what's important to them, we're simply throwing words against the wall and looking for something to stick. If we can put ourselves in their shoes and discover what's important to that crowd, we can tailor our message to something that cuts through and gets into their head. They can process that and say, "This is important, I want to learn more." It's targeting so that the message gets through to your target audience. It won't get through if they don't care.

Here's a real crisis I helped with which proves my point: We had issues with technology, not software and Internet, but the actual hardware, getting it to run a computer. There was a device called DRAM, Dynamic Random Access Memory.

There was a big political issue worldwide which had to do with Japan vs. US industry sanctions and tariffs. When I was brought into the situation, I took a look at what we were saying to the media at the time. The group I was working with was being skewered everyday, being taken apart, being blasted.

It was a negative story. I held a DRAM card in my hand and sat down with somebody from a television news show and said, "This is DRAM. This holds the information you put into your computer until you hit Save. It's important, and we need to clear up these marketing and international trade issues." It was an important point to get across because it switched how people perceived the story. Instead of us being the bad guys, we became the underdog. By understanding where people I was talking to were coming from, I was able to shift the conversation.

We live in a visual world. Some people learn through reading, others learn through seeing things, others learn from hearing things. If you're like my son, you need to move as you hear things -- motion and kinetic. Understand how people get their information and get it to them in that form.

Let me tell you why that's important: we have two seconds to make an impression on somebody. We have micro-expressions we exude without even being aware because they're not conscious. Someone sees those, perceives, and makes a decision. We're exposed to 34 gigabytes of information every day: 105,000 pages of copy and 7 hours of video. That's quite a bit of information to swim through to get to top-of-mind attention.

That's why it's important to target and understand your audience and bring the information from their perspective. What benefits them is one of the most important skills you can get as a communication.

That's the power of PR, Public Relations. You can parse your story to meet your audience. Years ago, I worked for Visa. We spoke to banks, doctors, and the public. I had the same story but took a different aspect of that story to media to reach those audiences. It looked like three different press releases, but it was all about the same story.

It was a program to help doctors with collecting their fees because at the time people didn't understand you could use your Visa card at the doctor. We spoke to doctors about us helping them manage their finances, and accounts, and they would get paid in 24 hours. We told banks how important it was to support this program and take it to their doctor customers because that not only helped their customers, but it also gave them an incremental sales boost which then helps their bottom line, their profits.

We worked hard at figuring out a good message for the public at large. We discovered that people were postponing doctor visits because they didn't have money to pay upfront. We positioned it as an option if they needed it -- go to the doctor and they take your Visa. That was one way to be able to get the care you need right away.

Customized speech is a skill we use every day. If you're in a family, you speak with your significant other at one level and your children differently. We must write at a five-year-old level these days to make explanations universally understandable. We naturally change our story and the perspective of our story based on who we're talking to.

We don't use certain words in front of little kids that we might use in front of young adults. I love to tease my clients about $50 words. When you pull out a word that's very much a piece of jargon that only people in your community understand and it's usually three or four syllables long, I smile and say, "That's a $50 word. Let's break it down because using that $50 jargon now cuts everybody out who is not in that community."

A real-world example is a billboard I used to drive by when I lived in Silicon Valley. It had a huge black bold word which said "Shockey" with a phone number. That's all it said. I asked my boss about it, and he said it was one of the most effective recruitment billboards he'd ever seen. If you were an engineer who knew about that technology, you'd call that phone number because it was a highly specialized technology.

It works both ways. If you want your story to get out to people, break up your audiences and market from different perspectives. Have a sales message for your sales targets, a business message for people you're reporting to, and a more general message to grab people that maybe interested in buying but aren't quite sure. It's the same story, just different aspects of it.

For most of us, nerdy details make our eyes glaze over, yet if we ask the person at the store for help, they can explain it. We are grateful because we can talk about different features.

When we have conversations, we typically want to get something done, but we're not specific on what our need is. You're having a conversation with a friend and want to make plans for a dinner. Decide which day you're available. Have a 20-minute conversation, but never ask that question.

Think about what you need to accomplish with that conversation. before you even start the conversation. Get together, talk and come up with a date, so you both walk away feeling like you've accomplished something. That moves your conversation forward.

Have an endpoint or goal. The end point could be having a conversation to catch up with somebody. That's a call to action. I have coffee with friends quite regularly to catch up and we might say we're putting the phones away so we're not interrupted. We then have 20 minutes to enjoy each other's company. That's a call to action. Making decisions like when to get together next, or what project we need help on. These are the things, if we take a moment and think about them, that help us become much more effective in our overall communication.

Make a decision, consciously or unconsciously, that you'll have a call to action to catch up and to figure out next steps. I say unconsciously because sometimes we're not even aware we've made a decision. I recently read about a study conducted by a major electronics conglomerate company. They studied their employees and concluded their employees were spending 17.5 hours per week unpacking miscommunications. Trying to figure out what their boss, and colleagues meant or what their customers needed. Simply because they weren't effective in their communication. That's not quite half of the work week. Another take is that explains why we're all working 60 to 80 hours per week, correcting mistakes.

Recapping communication is an acquired skill. Recap what was said, and then restate in a way that the person you are talking to understands. That's one of the ways to navigate conversations.

We've committed certain successful actions to muscle memory and don't think about them all that often. I call them superpowers, because once you think about them, you realize how important they are...

Superpower #1: Breathing. Most of us breathe shallowly in the top of our chest. We don't get the deep breath down in the belly.

When you breathe shallowly, your brain is caught fight-or-flight mode. It's enough to keep you alive. When you take a deep breath, your thought patterns move from fight-or-flight up into the logical frontal lobe where you can figure out what you need to say. When I train people for presentations and media interviews, I say it's the time when you engage your brain before opening your mouth.

It gives you a moment to ground yourself, decide what to say, and say it from a place of confidence. Breathing becomes important. When I work with executives and business leaders, I tell them to take that moment to ground themselves so they can handle anything thrown at them. Breathing becomes important in the day-to-day business world as well as in your everyday conversational world.

Superpower #2: Make a choice. Listen to somebody and in that moment, that's the stimulus. Choose how you'll respond. Will you react emotionally and make it chaotic or will you respond thoughtfully and deliberately? When somebody comes at you with road rage, you typically want to respond emotionally because that's our go-to.

When you take a deep breath and you're no longer in fight or flight, you choose. You could say there is a mistake, apologize, and walk away. Change the energy in the room responding to something. You could walk in with a big smile on your face because you chose to be high energy and the room moves with you, or you could choose to be tired and low energy and the room sucks the rest out of you. It's a very important power to choose how you will act or react.

Superpower #3: Listen. For the most part, we all believe we listen. In conversation, you naturally listen to the first sentence or two, and automatically, you think about how to respond. It's human nature. You enter the file cabinets in your mind to see what you can pull up.

While you're doing that, you're not hearing the rest of the conversation. You miss out on half, and that's where miscommunication occurs. Steve Harvey, host of Family Feud, begins to say, "According to 100 people surveyed, the best room in the house is..." You tap the buzzer. "The best room in the house is..." is what you must answer. You don't know the complete question.

That's what we do in many conversations. We don't hear the whole issue before we begin to respond. When you hear that voice asking what to say, train yourself to put that aside and focus on what your conversation partner is saying, then recap. "I understand what you're saying, but let's move the conversation over here."

That's where listening is important. You can't solve a problem if you don't know what the problem is. It's one of the most difficult ones because literally every single person I've talked to says they listen, but we only hear half.

If you listen hard and still don't understand, ask questions. We want to feel like we know everything, but we're afraid to ask questions. We don't want to seem stupid, but that's not reality. We have so much coming at us, it's hard to process all the information.

Could you imagine if you sat down to watch the seven hours of video and 105,000 pages of information being thrown out you daily? You'd never get anything done. That's a Stephen King novel. How many people can read a Stephen King novel every day and still be on top of things?

Superpower skills need to be practiced. We practice riding a bike or playing golf. These take two, three, or four actions at once, and it becomes muscle memory. That's why we don't pay attention to what's no longer important. Practice listening, choosing and breathing so that it becomes part of your muscle memory to make it easier to become an effective communicator.

Practice and muscle memory are important. I didn't ride a bike for 10 years, but getting back into it was natural. It's the same with communication.

Next Steps

1. Have you identified a skill that's easy for you but extraordinary to others?

2. Have you recently thought about your audience's wants and needs?

3. What visual component can you implement in your presentations to better make your point?

4. Do you take deep breaths instead of shallow ones? (superpower #1)

5. From now on, in difficult situations, will you make a conscious decision about how to act or react? (superpower #2)

6. Do you practice attentive listening, and ask questions if you don't understand? (superpower #3)

Jeanne's Contact Information

- Website: AlfordCommunications.com

- E-book: Three Magic Questions to Instantly Improve Communications

- Book: Bloom Where You are Planted and Shine compiled by Rebecca Hall Gruyter

Chapter 6: Live Long and Stay Productive At Any Age by Renee Balcom

Renee Balcom is a certified community health worker and an adjunct professor who lives in Oregon. She knows a lot about elder care and ran a business which provided health advocacy and care management services. We will all be old eventually and we might

have those family members that who need that extra little bit of help, so it's always good to know what we'll need to know at a certain age.

I'm an adjunct professor in the Los Rios Community College district. We're launching a program to certify community health workers. Community health workers have a little bit of an identity crisis because they fall under a variety of different titles. The community health worker is part of an outreach team, they do health advocacy, they're usually health educators and health ambassadors. You'll see them at health fairs. They work in clinics and in hospital settings and are part of the continuum of care provided for individuals and for patients. They do a variety of different work.

They're valuable in the healthcare system because it's a low-cost liaison from the patient to the provider. They help patients maneuver through the various health care and social services systems. I coordinate and teach that brand-new program we're launching in the fall.

My background: I worked in Oregon as a community health worker. I owned a business there and employed 29 community health workers in Southwest Oregon. I was also seated by Governor John Kitzhaber at the time and helped write the scope of certification for the community health worker for the state of Oregon and chaired that committee at a state level. In Oregon we have state certifications but in California we don't have a state certification process yet. We'll see where that goes on a political road, but for now, we're doing a local educational certification at the college level.

Healthcare workers have different specialties. I'm a personal, professional health advocate. I work specifically with individuals to help them maneuver through the healthcare system.

Let's say you were diagnosed with cancer and were in need of a specialist. When you have a severe diagnosis or become chronically ill, you have difficulty processing through the information and possible choices. A professional health advocate or community health worker comes alongside to assist you in sorting through the information. They help you make the health decisions right for you. They can assist in getting the right specialist, documentation and paperwork lined up.

I provide that service as a community health worker. I'm also a billing specialist. Because of numerous changes in billing codes, nine out of ten medical bills are incorrect, up to at least 25%. If you have a $1,000 medical bill, you can count on overpaying it by $250. I provide a service to review those bills, then negotiate issues and mistakes away.

I worked in technology for 25 years in the Bay area, and in 2001 I became semi-retired and moved to Oregon. I soon realized that retirement wasn't in the cards for me. I went back to work in our small county and realized there were big gaps in healthcare in peoples' ability to access care and support. I started with one client at a time, then found myself servicing several clients in our county and two other adjacent counties in southwest Oregon working to assist people in navigating the healthcare systems.

I've been asked what that transition was like, going from technology to healthcare, and the similarities are amazing. Healthcare is multilayered and fast moving. We need to bring technology and people like myself that are fast movers into the healthcare system. I found it to be an easy transition to move into the support system of healthcare. From there, I pursued my certifications and started working to make certain I had the credentials I needed and launched a second career.

I don't believe in retirement. There's always something to do with our skills and our talents. Lounging around and exploring hobbies wasn't for me. My hobbies were working with my neighbors and getting acquainted with my community. It didn't take me long to find myself back in a service business environment.

My plan at some point is to do standup comedy. When I get into my 70's, the world will need a funny old lady. My goal is to have several more careers as I age.

When I left technology and I began working with individuals and healthcare, I became aware of the gaps and deficits we have in our culture and that people need a hand up. They need someone to come along side of them and help them. It wasn't difficult to find a space where I could use the experience I acquired in Silicon Valley. Because I was a president of a tech company there, it wasn't difficult to find the space to take those talents, gifts and experience and apply it into helping my community and reaching out to other people. I'm sometimes invited to speak to groups.

Reach out to your neighbors, even if you are a stay-at-home mom or are retired. Be certain you're checking in on the people who live near you. Ensure and they get the support they need. You'll find someone that needs your help, whether it's a ride to the doctor or grocery store, to pick up an item or keep an eye on their dog while they vacation. We are a community of people living amongst each other and we need each other. In that effort, you'll find a new calling in life. Personally, I've decided that retirement is not part of my life.

I might have a while until I get to standup comedy. I'm a serial entrepreneur, and I'm toying with the idea of a script for a television show. You must find the humor when you work with people, and I've met some unbelievable amazing ones. I want to document those experiences. A book or television show could shine a spotlight on the information and education we need.

I'm an early riser. I start the day in my home office around 4:00 am. It gives me time to get focused and focus my day. That's also a time where I use a lot of writing time because the world is quiet in the morning. I block off parts of my calendar for specific tasks. The part of the work that I do with the college is part-time work. It doesn't require a 40-hour week. I finish that work in less than 20 hours a week, which opens up opportunities for health advocacy work and speaking work.

Look at your calendar. Block off times and commit to those times and tasks you want to put into those blocks. That's how I manage my time. I usually don't work too much on weekends. I'm committed to a Monday through Friday work week, but I seem to be able to manage my time that way.

I block off three hours in the morning for writing, focusing on classwork, creating a PowerPoint presentations. After 8:00 I have personal quiet time and get myself together. Once I'm ready to go out into the world, I meet with clients. I'll schedule client appointments in the morning between 10:00 and 2:00. I may do community work later in the afternoon. I may also be meeting practitioners and doing work with potential referral sources later in the day.

It can be hard to ensure you block off the correct amount of time for specific tasks. There have been times when I've blocked out my calendar with tasks, but didn't have enough time in the day to complete everything. I've had to learn how to edit and determine the tasks I need to complete, write them down, prioritize, and then use my calendar efficiently. We move through tasks differently. Experiment with this.

It's also important to leave room for flexibility. The best plans can often times be upset. Forgive yourself, and give yourself some flexibility. Sometimes, I look at my calendar and know things are getting busy. I block off down time, knowing that I must take care of myself to deal with the overwhelm.

Quiet time is important. I used to get out of bed and jump right into my day. I was not as productive. Roll out of bed, hurrying up to get dressed, and sitting in traffic is not as productive as taking 15 minutes to center yourself. Taking that time to check in and know with purpose how you want your day to unfold.

I love visualizing the necessary tasks that I'm about to complete. Once you visualize it, you can march right through certain things.

Some people claim productivity becomes more difficult as they age. I have not had that experience. We're different physiologically. It's important to take care of ourselves. I've worked with hundreds of elders age 90 and above. The healthiest ones pace themselves and do everything in moderation. Most of them don't withhold anything they want from themselves, but they do everything moderately. They get good sleep and make certain they get exercise.

I had a 101-year-old client who took a walk every day. They move their bodies and make certain they're taking in a good amount of fluids and clear waters. You don't have to go into a wheelchair or walker. Move through your life with vitality and energy. There's misinformation in our culture about aging. Look forward to growing older.

I'm 60 years old, but as I'm processing through my life I have more clarity. I understand things that are more important to me now than they were before. I'm not in a world of acquisition anymore, so I don't need to acquire anything new. I have what I need. I know that's different for people that are younger who are still in the acquiring mode, but if you take care of yourself moderately, you will have all the clarity you need if you're healthy.

Based on today's number, the average male will live to age 84 and the average female will live to 87.

Life Tip #1: Get a health advocate. I have a young 25-year-old client who was recently diagnosed with early stage cervical cancer. She's a beautiful, healthy, amazing woman. She is in the gym every day, eats well, and takes good care of herself. Her diagnosis came up a week ago. What happens is you get very myopic and you're afraid. Move through the healthcare system. You're fearful of the next step, what other information you'll hear about.

She hired me to come alongside her as a health advocate and assist her in those appointments and make certain she understands what the doctor's order is, to assist her through her treatments, and make certain she's got all the support. Maybe a nutritionist will come in and prepare meals for her and make certain she's getting everything she needs for her wellbeing and overall health. I encourage everyone who is in the healthcare system or has a medical issue or a loved one that has a medical issue to look at getting a health advocate. It's a low-cost assistant in processing through the system.

Life Tip #2: Avoid white coat syndrome when visiting the doctor. We all have a little bit of that. It's common for us to simply tell the doctor, "I'm okay." Most of us were brought up with the advice, "If you can't say something nice, don't say anything." We expect the doctor to understand what's going on with us, but we often don't articulate ourselves and explain our needs. There's a patient-doctor communication gap.

Write down the points you need to make to your doctor. Take those notes in with you to the doctor and make certain you're touching on every point. When we get in front of the doctor, often times, we forget or our mind goes into a different space. We experience fear, white coat syndrome, and don't always articulate ourselves. Once we leave, we think, "I wish I would have told the doctor THIS." Have a good, organized meeting and communication with your doctor. Use a health advocate if you're in a critical situation or if you are very sick, or if you're dealing with a severe diagnosis. The other low hanging fruit is, as we work with the aging population, it's important to make certain they're getting the care supports they need. We have a lot of aging people driving cars that shouldn't be driving anymore and are afraid to surrender their licenses because how will they get to the grocery store? How will they get to the doctor? There are lots of services coming up now available to assist our sick and aging population. I encourage people to go out and learn about those services.

Life Tip #3: It's okay to ask questions when visiting your medical provider. Doctors are tasked to see a patient every 10 minutes. If your schedule involved talking to a different person every 10 minutes, your brain would be in multitasking overload.

It's okay when the doctor comes into the room for you to say, "Can you sit down with me and talk to me about a few things?" I promise you when you do that the doctor's almost relieved for the patients to take a little bit more control of their appointments and ask for a few minutes of their time to talk. I encourage people to step into their healthcare and take the initiative with practitioners. Pace your own appointments and you'll find they are relieved that you do.

Take care of yourself. I don't charge a fee for my medical billing service, unless it saves the client money. It's a free service. I take 25% of every dollar I save. Example: if I save you $250, you pay me $50 to do that.

If you're in the Sacramento region and you need a health advocate or you need a medical bill examined, make a quick phone call to me at 541-661-2369. See if I can help you out. There's no downside in asking for help, but there is a downside in being a little shy or maybe a little arrogant and trying to do it all yourself. (That seems like an easy recipe to drive yourself crazy.) Reach out for that extra help and have a quick conversation with me to see if I can help you out with your current situation.

Next Steps

1. Do you wake up early and block off quiet time on your calendar to get important work done?

2. Do you practice any form of visualization to further solidify your goals?

3. Can you verify that you do things in moderation? Do you get good sleep and exercise?

Renee's Contact Information

- LinkedIn: LinkedIn.com/in/reneebalcom

- Phone: 541-661-2369 (if you're close to Sacramento, California, USA, call for the medical billing review service)

- Email: renee@reneecompany.com

- Website: ReneeCompany.com

Chapter 6: Live Long and Stay Productive At Any Age by Renee Balcom

Chapter 7: Break Outside Your Comfort Zone by Philip Williams

Philip Williams is a three-time Inc 5000 honoree, after becoming the CEO of a 17-year-old cash strapped company and growing it at 50% per year for five straight years. Philip has bought and sold a couple companies, and has been through those highs and lows you can only experience through small business ownership. Philip helps small business owners build profitable and well-respected companies through his consulting.

I've been asked, "How did you get rolling from being cash strapped?" We funded our entire business from cashflow, no outside money. I'm a goal-oriented person, but I didn't give any single employee in my business a written goal until I had been there over two years.

This was a geophysical consulting firm. We did a lot of work for large architectural and engineering firms, mining companies, utilities and industries like that. If they had a bad environmental problem, we would go in and essentially define how bad it was, then hand it off to them, and they'd have to clean it up.

There wasn't much margin for error. In the very early days, I'd been onboard four weeks. One of our senior project managers walked into the office, and said, "I got off the phone with a utility in another state, and they're in bad shape. The Department of Environmental Quality is breathing down their neck, and they need to have somebody come in and help them out." They were willing to pay double, but I told him we were so booked up, I wasn't sure that we could do it.

That was a turning point. I said, "Nobody's shown me we can't fit it in. How about we meet in an hour? In an hour, I want to see every upcoming project for the next three months, who's on it, what resources are needed and what the timing is. Let's write it on a whiteboard and see if we can fit it in." We met an hour later and spent 45 minutes whiteboarding and made it fit. That project is the project which saved that year because, we were going to grow 40%, but we would be paying our clients to grow that much. We were not going to be doing it profitably, and we made it fit in.

That client came back to us again and again with several other problems, and they were always willing to pay very good money to have us go. One of the hardest things a company has to deal with when they're trying to learn how to grow is getting outside of what's comfortable and understanding how to coach the team in a way that shows them it's okay. If you've been stuck in your comfy shoes for a while, that can be very difficult.

No company has perfectly smooth revenue. You might be doing a million bucks a year, $83,000 per month. The easiest way to figure out what your company can do at any given moment is go back and look at the last year, and find your three or four best revenue months. You have a few months that were $100,000, $105,000, $110,000, and ugly months. Your company over the last year has produced three or four months that were in the $105,000 neighborhood. That's what your company is capable of on a consistent basis at this exact moment with what they know how to do. Go back to your team and talk about how that's where you want the company to be. Don't talk about it in terms of, "I want to hit $105,000." Nobody buys into your company. Nobody comes to work every day because they love your balance sheet.

They come to work because they know they love what you do. Whether you're selling bridal gowns, T-shirts or widgets, talk about it in terms of serving that number of clients. When you look at your $105,000 months, the two, three or four months that you've had over the last year, what did that translate to? How many clients were you serving? Talk about your company mission in terms of supporting that number of clients, on a consistent basis.

Ask your team two questions: first, what three or four things did we do right, to make those "winning" months possible? Second, how did you shoot yourself in the foot during your two or three "worst" months last year? Ask your team, "How did we do that?

Why was it so miserable in those down months? How can we stop doing that?"

Focus on three things. How do we support more clients every month in our mission? If you sell bridal gowns, you want your team to feel like any bride that walks down the aisle who isn't wearing a gown sold in your shop was cheated. That's how you want everybody to feel.

Everyone should be thinking about the things they do correctly, that make it possible to serve more brides, and stop doing the things that shoot themselves in the foot. Get your team working on those three items and you will break your business out of the doldrums, moving in the direction you want to go. Continually move through that exercise until you develop this cultural expectation.

Let's say the number turns out that, "We can grow 20% next year." After you've done that once, you go back to your team and say, "Hey guys, we want to keep doing that. We are a company that can grow at 20% per year, we proved that. How do we do it again?" Go back and again, you look at your best three or four months. What happens is you develop this cultural expectation, this baseline that, "We're the team that does this. This is what we do." Next thing you know, when you're hiring a new guy and he's in the lunch room getting the breakdown from the team when you're not around on day two, the story he or she gets told is, "This is what we do. This is how we do it. This is who we are." It becomes a much more positive story and you don't have to sweat that.

Many times, as a leader, you hire someone to help change your company culture, and it's not fair to treat the new person that way. Don't expect them to do all the cultural lifting. Do it as a leader.

When you do it in the way I suggested, it becomes easier. We grew 50% that first year. I set the next year's goal to 50%. I was able to look at the team and say, "Hey guys, you did this. This is what you did. This wasn't Phil's dream, this is what you delivered. I believe that your team can do it again and again."

I'm a big fan of not taking myself too seriously, and I like to poke fun at and learn from my mistakes. In the early 1900's, Thomas Watson from IBM experienced many legal troubles. If you want to double your successes, double your failures. If you want your team to feel comfortable sticking their neck out, help and understand them when they fail.

When your two-year-old falls down while learning to walk, your response is to pick them up, hug them, dust them off, and let them know that it's okay to move forward again. As long as you don't lose a customer, hurt somebody or bankrupt the company, you can learn from any mistake.

Our company created an annual award called the Huggy. At the end-of-year company Christmas party, everyone (including me) wins a "Huggy" -- a celebration of that person's biggest screw up that year.

My worst mistake was a painful lesson: we had an employee who was hurt on a job site through no fault of his own. He followed every safety protocol, and the audit showed he did nothing wrong. The client was pleased we were able to show the employee did nothing wrong, but my mistake was not calling the client fast enough. That's an important safety tip to leaders out there: if your team messes up, make that call. My perspective at the time was, "My team was handling it. I was getting good feedback. I heard the right things." The client wanted to hear from ME.

One simple phone call would have helped them quite a bit. We didn't lose the client, but the client was frustrated that I didn't call sooner. I called four or five days later, but they wanted to hear from me that day.

As leaders, we want to support and help our team. My team felt supported, and that they had control, but the client was unhappy that I didn't call fast enough. As a leader, eat that Humble Pie. Reach out and call the client. Don't step on your employees toes. Let your employees know, "I'll make this phone call because this is important."

It's easy to fall in love with your "widget" or your way of doing things and ignore what your client wants. These days, that's called Blockbuster Video.

Let's talk about Greg Lamont's 1989 2,041-mile Tour de France win. The race ended on a 15-mile time trial solo race. One rider on the course was released every two minutes. You'd never see another rider, but were cranking out 15 miles as hard and fast as you could.

The last day of this 15-mile race, after riding 2,025 miles, Greg LeMond was down by 50 seconds. Every expert was sure he wouldn't win, so the French newspapers printed editions ahead of time stating that Fignon, the Frenchman leading at the time, won the Tour de France.

The night before the race, LeMond and his team strategized about what to do to make sure the bike was ready to go. He placed a narrow Time Trial handlebar on his bike. He wore a long bullet shaped helmet, and placed the bike in a tall gear, 55x12. At those settings, you'd feel like you were squatting 200 pounds every time you turned the crank.

He set his bike up to go as fast as humanly possible. Fignon began first, with a wide handle bar, no helmet, a long brown ponytail flowing behind, cranking at a world class speed. He crossed the line at 33.5 miles per hour, a solid performance.

It was LeMond's turn to ride the race. He called a team manager and said, "I don't want to see anybody on the team calling my time splits." In a Time Trial, they would normally have somebody on the track every two or three miles yelling out to LeMond where he stood.

LeMond continued, "I don't want to see anyone with a stopwatch yelling my time to me. If I don't ride my absolute best, for the entire 15 miles, this doesn't matter. There's no way I can beat him if I am not at my absolute peak, every turn of the crank, every single meter on this track. Don't call out the times. It won't matter if I'm not doing my best." 15.5 miles later, 2,041 miles, over 18 of those days were 100-plus miles per day, LeMond crossed the finish line at 34.4 miles an hour. He rode a 2,041 mile race to beat his competitor by eight seconds.

The night before, everyone had written him off. That day, he simply focused on everything he needed to be at his best. Fignon didn't matter. LeMond focused on being his best in that 15 miles. He cut 58 seconds off Fignon's time, good enough to win a 2,041 mile race by all of eight seconds.

The relevance to that story: many companies are trying to beat the competition. LeMond wasn't trying to beat the competition. His goal was to perform at his absolute best with every turn of the crank.

If you're running a company, don't worry about competition. Be your best on Monday, Tuesday, Wednesday, Thursday. In two or three years, you will be the apex predator in your company or market. Don't worry about the competition. Do what you must to be at your best every day, and avoid shooting yourself in the foot three or four times per year. Focus on what causes you to have the best months, and you will win the race.

I have a 3x5 note card listing my six lifetime events, where I started slow, started from behind, and won. I have not been the underdog only one time. It's happened many times. I have six specific life events where I've been the underdog, and in the end, finished on top.

It's easy to find AND believe the negative press about yourself, internally, or from people who throw stones at you. However, everyone has had some form of success in their life. Take a three by five card and list your successes in ink. Even leaders have down moments, and unfortunately, you don't have as many people to speak with as the folks that work for you. If you have that card, you can sit down and say, "This is another one of those times where I'm the underdog. I've been here before, and I've always bounced back." If you can remind yourself of that, it's a useful tool.

When it's written in black and white, you can't ignore it. That circles back to my earlier goal setting strategy, teaching self-belief to your team. Look the team's delivered accomplishments and discuss their successes. When you look at the successes you've had and you're using that tool to build yourself up, as well as using that method to build your team, it is truly useful.

In psychology, it's called self-efficacy theory. Self-beliefs are self-fulfilling prophecies. Whether you choose to believe the good or bad is up to you. Tony Robbins has built an empire teaching people how to believe in the good. Take that simple approach and direct it at your team and yourself. It's very useful. On a three by five index card, list the five or six times you've been an underdog and finished strongly. When you feel down, read that card.

I typically deal with companies that have at least six or seven employees. That's the very first time the ownership is searching for a right-hand man. They're dealing with the complexities and issues involved in having an organization, and they're handing off a few things and having to deal with the nervousness of letting a right-hand man handle it when they're not in the shop. Up to about 50 employees.

I can go into a business, figure out how to make it tick, and make it go faster. That's why I chose this path of coaching companies. I love helping ownership see a unique goal setting strategy. I help them find ways to coach their teams on self-belief.

I've worked with many businesses: professional services, manufacturing, blue collar services, engineering consulting. I come in, sit down and talk with everybody. I take a full look at the hard and soft components.

I have a set of questions that help me figure out where a business does not run the way the owner says it does. I can work that out for you, and get the hard numbers of the business adjusted. If you were to bring a new CEO into your company, he or she would have an approach to analyzing the business that is both hard and soft. If you sold your company after 10 years of running it successfully, the acquirer would look at very hard numbers. I've molded those two processes together to develop a way of figuring out a company very quickly, and helping the leadership figure how they can improve. Three or four things to work on now, plus three or four things to stop doing.

Next Steps

1. Have you examined your 3-4 best months last year to determine what actions led to that, and how many clients you served?

2. Have you also checked your 2-3 worst months last year to uncover what actions and habits led you there?

3. What three critical elements can you and your team completely focus on to achieve success?

4. Can you create a 3x5 note card and list the 6 "wins" in your life?

Philip's Contact Information

- AskPhilipWilliams.com (official site)

- LinkedIn: LinkedIn.com/in/Philip-Williams

- Twitter: @askphilipw

Chapter 8: Build an Online Business Through Content Marketing by Bernie Thompson

Bernie Thompson has founded five companies, including the global electronics brand, Plugable. He's also the founder of Efficient Era, a company that helps other companies sell on Amazon. He's an engineer and an inventor with four patents, and he considers

marketing his greatest weakness, so we'll hear all kinds of interesting stories and lessons.

One of the things about not being a professional marketer is we've done it in a lot of non-traditional ways, which are somewhat interesting to talk about.

I'm a software engineer by background. I've worked at a bunch of big companies including IBM and Microsoft, in operating system development, which is the lowest level tech there is. I've built a few companies. Plugable is a global electronics brand with 120 products sold in North America, Europe and Japan. Here's what's interesting: we did not have a full time marketing specialist working with the company at all for the first seven years of its existence. We marketed in a different way (content marketing) and tried to reach a narrower but more interested audience through YouTube and content. To summarize the process, we had a content marketing strategy.

If you're selling a product right now in the United States, you must be on Amazon. That's a big part of what we do. If you're selling a service or something similar, there's a lot of service lists that you'll want to be on and review sites are invaluable. The good thing about that is they allow you to focus on your business, product or service. They'll do a bit of basic marketing for you if you're doing your job well, but you can accelerate that with some additional good marketing strategies.

YouTube has been our best marketing channel. We have about 10,000 YouTube subscribers at this point, which are all organic. That 10,000 has grown very slowly over the life of the company along with several million video views. Some products are relatively simple, but you need to see them in context. Our products tend to be complicated and interesting. They enable you to do exciting things that aren't always obvious, so, for example, we demonstrate connecting a docking station with a USB port in video form. I used to think USB ports were for mice. I can now connect a docking station, get extra monitors, connect hard drives and have a clean desk setup with this amazing set of functionalities, connected using a single USB port."

People need to see what works and how to do it. With our USB products, which are the more interesting, high-function docking station, adapter type USB products, we need to show our potential customers what we can do. Once they see it, they say, "I didn't realize I could do that. I want that."

It's surprising how hard it is to find that one specific solution potential consumers may need. As a technologist, it's easy for me to tick off the features, but it's hard for me to translate that into specific audiences and the specific benefits that those audiences want, because I need to do what I'm not good at, solid marketing. I have to do my customer analysis and try to break things down in ways that make sense and try to articulate benefits that I might not even care about or see. It's surprisingly hard to do it well.

We talk about that challenge of focusing on features or benefits. How can we better break this down into audiences, and benefits, rather than products and features? Especially as we head beyond the video, into marketing the video or doing any keyword advertising to our products. We can be more effective if we've nailed that breakdown and have correctly identified an audience that has a similar worldview about something. We then look at how that same audience would articulate their problem and what possible benefit or outcome they are hoping for. This will give us the words they are using in their search, aka keywords. We have gotten better at it over the years, but I still feel like there is a lot of room for improvement. It's surprisingly hard. It's so hard that you almost can't do it without having a strategy in place. Look at the data, refine your audiences and your messages.

Our strategy for driving traffic to the YouTube videos so far has been to post it, look for an organic response and then double down where we see traction. "Doubling down" means spending ad dollars. The root of that is we don't know which of the videos will catch fire. We'll post a video we think is so super informative, or clever, and it might turn out to be a dud and no one reacts to it. We then try to push traffic to it, but there's no reaction. There will be another video where we just think it's one of our normal ones and it catches people's attention. They want to share it.

In recent years, we have grown enough of an audience that we have a good sampling of viewership by simply posting a video. We'll gauge the reaction of that set. They're probably our fans, our regular viewers. We'll see how our fans react, and if our fans like it, we'll start spending ad dollars on it.

When we've been at our best, we have posted one to two videos per week. There's definitely a lot of chatter about what pace of video output you need to get rewards from the algorithms and to keep your fans engaged. We think that's probably the minimum. It's hard to discern. In recent months we've fallen way behind that pace, so there's been an awareness that we're failing to take full advantage of the opportunity we have, especially once we've built an audience.

As we've built up a catalog of YouTube videos, we think some things are going on with Google's algorithms for YouTube search. If we're posting regularly, we have more activity in our whole catalog of videos, by way of people commenting and liking, even going back in time. If we let our new videos trail off, the overall activity in our whole catalog drops off. That may be in direct relation to what we try to do at the end of each video, which is highlight a few of our other videos. Google does that within the YouTube interface. They show other similar videos, often yours. Whatever it is cumulatively, from an algorithm perspective, it feels like a snowball effect. Add to that snowball so that it rolls faster.

Finding the balance between quantity vs. quality can be daunting. We often have internal conflicts about whether or not we have a quality bar. What is our quality bar for videos? I've been an advocate and have a team working for me. We have some employees empowered to create videos. If they have a topic that relates to our products that they want to do a video on, that's their ball to run with. We don't put a lot of gatekeepers in the way that have to approve or disapprove things.

Someone on our customer service team will publish videos focused around a common problem they see among our customer base, and how to solve it. Other people create videos geared toward the marketing sector, while I focus on educational videos. One of the most effective types of videos we do is where a big company introduces a new laptop. Apple will produce a new MacBook, for example. We'll show our latest products along with Apple's latest products.

We've got a lot of different videos done by various people and done to different quality levels. It's worked for us. There's an argument that we're not maintaining a very controlled brand image by letting that diversity occur, but that it's worked for us.

The end result: our fans see new videos. Some think, "That's a support video. I'll pass on that. Here's a video showing how to make the most of the new MacBook. I'll watch that." They become familiar with our styles that we have and decide what resonates.

Another company is Efficient Era, which spun off from Plugable. When Plugable started as an electronics company in 2009, we made a bet on Amazon. We wanted to focus solely on products, education about the products and support of the products. We didn't want to bother with marketing, sales or logistics. At the time of the bet, it wasn't clear who would win: Amazon or eBay. It turned out to be a great bet, because Amazon has eaten everybody's lunch in the years since 2009.

When betting on Amazon, we developed software to help us sell on that platform. It centers around focusing on the customer and their feedback. We're grabbing data from Amazon's systems, the APIs and the website, to ensure we, as a seller of products, know everything that's happening with those products.

For example, when someone submits a positive or negative review of our products, we want to be notified immediately. If the review is negative, we want to help the customer with the issue that caused them to leave a negative review. If the review is positive, that is something we might publicize or Tweet about.

We initially created this as internal software for ourselves, and Amazon exploded, so maintaining the software for one single company was no longer cost effective. We needed to offer it to other sellers to justify the cost of running a great system to sell on Amazon. That's Efficient Era.

If you're an Amazon seller, we offer a month-long trial for you to try our features. We take everything Amazon offers you as a seller and go beyond in each area: reviews, email communication with customers, viewing listings, running ads. We handle the nitty-gritty customer service details, for example, invoicing in Europe. It evolved from problems we originally solved for ourselves.

We've been happy with Efficient Era. We now have over 200 Amazon sellers using the software. It's complex, but we live in Amazon's ecosystem. Amazon solves problems all day long, often first for themselves, then they break those down into services and offer to other consumers. We're mirroring the Jeff Bezos model of finding an unsolved problem (often, one that is your own), and turning each one into its own micro-business. Not everybody can do it and you must wait for the right opportunity. We now have two different revenue sources that are diversified and can help make the company more stable.

Next Steps

1. If you sell a physical product, is it listed on Amazon?

2. Do you have a YouTube channel and have you posted a video there in the last 30 days?

3. What marketing "demo" can you record to show off one of your products on YouTube?

4. What common problem with your customers can you solve with a YouTube video?

5. What educational video can you create that shows your product in action?

6. Will you commit to regularly checking your audience numbers and YouTube stats?

Bernie's Contact Information

- Plugable.com (USB devices)

- EfficientEra.com (resources for Amazon sellers)

Chapter 9: Write Your Book in a Flash by Dan Janal

Dan Janal helps leaders build their brands with books. Dan has written more than a dozen books and his latest book is called Write Your Book in a Flash: The Paint by Numbers System for Writing the Book of Your Dreams Fast.

I'm into systems. I believe in creating the easiest path. As a newspaper reporter or journalist, we had to write the same stories over and over: traffic accidents, obituaries, board meetings, and those all fall into a similar pattern. Once you realize the pattern, it's easy. You're filling in the blanks.

I've written 13 books, and my latest is Write Your Book in a Flash: The Paint by Numbers System to Write the Book of Your Dreams Fast.

Think back to when you were in the third, fourth, or fifth grade, when you graduated from finger painting and your mother got you the paint by numbers system. You saw this outline, a picture of a farm.

There was a barn and there were cows and there was a sky and there was grass, but it was all white. There were outlines for the cow and inside that outline, the cow was labeled with a number. Number six because six was brown. We had brown cows. You took your "brown" color, the number six pencil, and shaded in the cow. You left blank white spots because cows have white spots.

You'd look at the sky on your paint-by-numbers drawing and think, "I'll color a dark blue sky or a light blue sky." Some days, you'd look at it and say, "There's a lot to do and I don't feel like working on that. I want something simple." You'd do something simple instead.

That's my analogy for writing your book. If you have a deep, textured outline for your book, you have the same outline that you have for your paint by numbers picture.

Look at that outline every day and say, "I'm feeling sluggish today, I want to do something simple. I'll get quotes from famous people at BrainyQuote.com, and I'll add those in front of each chapter of my book." Another day, you might say, "I have more energy and lots of notes. I'll tackle that chapter that was previously daunting."

That gets your book done. Similar to the paint by numbers picture, you can have a book done in a very short period of time if you have a good outline.

People need a system in place because they lose momentum. That's why many people don't write their books. I'm advocating not only the outline, but there's more in the book than just how to create a good outline. I have a whole chapter on how to overcome the limiting beliefs which stop you from writing your book because, let's face it, writing is the only profession in the world that has built in excuses.

"I have writer's block, I can't write today." Have you heard of ditch digger's block? No, the guys who dig ditches have to dig ditches every day whether their back hurts or they have a migraine. They're digging ditches every day. Somehow, writers think they can take a day off and not do it because they're not in the mood.

I have a chapter that debunks many of those myths, gives you some NLP techniques, some other ideas that get people over that hump because it's only human nature. It happens to all of us. I'm joking about the ditch diggers thing and the writer's block. It happens, but it doesn't need to happen. I'd like to make a special offer to everyone if they go to my website, WriteYourBookInAFlash.com. Download a free chapter from the book on how to overcome all the limiting beliefs, and believe me, I've heard all of them. There are foolproof methods for overcoming those things to get your energy back up and get you over that hump to write your book.

Naysayer perfectionists will never finish their book because it's never good enough. There's an old saying, "Good is good enough and perfection is the enemy of done." There are many similar sayings to get you over the hump. People don't have confidence in what they are saying.

They either need to do more research so they feel more confident about their material, and let's face it, many of us have the imposter syndrome. Even the most successful people in the world have what's called the imposter syndrome and I address that in my book as well. Overcome it by doing more research and becoming smarter so you feel more confident or get beta readers, peer reviewers.

Other people read your chapters or your book and tell you what they like, what they didn't like, what's missing or what could be made better. When you click the print, publish or CreateSpace button, or the "Send It to Your Publisher" button, you're confident that you've done the best job possible and other people agree with you. That would be one tactic for getting over the syndrome which stops a lot of people from finishing their books.

Another option: work with a coach. I work with many authors. The coach sees things you don't see. They help you with imposter syndrome and help you get over the humps. They also see what's missing. I remember working with one woman who wrote a book about improv for nurses and doctors. She said if you used improv techniques, you would improve communications between doctors and nurses, and experience fewer problems. I thought, "That's a great idea for a book."

She had an example of dialogue of a conversation gone bad. The nurse would say one thing and the doctor would fly off the handle and act horribly. She said, "You can rectify the situation if you used this improv technique." She described the technique, but didn't have a sample dialog showing a good interaction -- what you could expect as a result of using this improv technique. When I pointed that out to her, she said, "You're absolutely right. That makes the book so much better."

Work with a book coach who can help you mentally get over those humps as well as look at your manuscript and see how it could be made better. No one writes a book alone anymore. We think it's a solitary process, and for the most part it is, but those are not the books that are so great. The books that are great have a team behind them.

Ken Blanchard wrote "The One Minute Manager" and "Who Moved My Cheese", and he's sold 62 million copies of books. He's written 25 books, and I interviewed him for my book. I asked, "Why do you collaborate? You own your books with co-authors." He said, "Because I get so much smarter when I work with somebody else." I thought that was powerful that someone as well published and smart as he is is still so humble to realize he doesn't know it all. Other people have expertise and value they can lend to a project to make his book better and help the world become a better place. It's nice to be humble and follow Ken Blanchard's role model. He knows something about writing books.

How much information do you need to share? Many people think, "I need to write the encyclopedia about my topic." I have news for you. No one wants to read an encyclopedia about this topic. The purpose of the book, especially for entrepreneurs, coaches, consultants, speakers, and thought leaders, is to act as a big business card. It's a way for your prospects to get to know, like and trust you so they want to do business with you. If you figure out what their big problem is, they'll want to read the book. The only reason anyone will read or buy a book is to solve a problem.

The first step: ask yourself, what is my ideal client's problem? I'll write 10 chapters showing I have solved that problem, and I have stories and examples from other clients I've worked with explaining how I solved that problem.

When that "ideal client" reads that book, he's read it cover-to-cover during a single airplane flight from New York to Los Angeles, because the book is thin. It's 120 pages -- 20,000 to 25,000 words. It doesn't look intimidating. It's not three inches thick. It's half an inch thick. Someone who sees your book will think, "I can get through this. This looks like an interesting read. I wonder what he or she has to say that can help me." That's what your book needs to be about.

Work with a single-minded purpose: get that ideal client to know, like and trust you as their guide who can help them solve their problems, so they want to retain you and your very high (but reasonable) coaching/consulting fees, and want to hire you. That's the purpose of the book.

There are two ways to write a book in a flash. First, you can write it and you can transcribe it. Take your blog posts you've already written over the last year or two and reformat them so those become a book. You don't have to create any new content in that case, or you might have new transitions or introductions or bring some things that are two years old up to date, and you have your book.

You might be speaking a lot, or have many webinars and podcasts. You have transcripts for those events. Why not take those transcripts and turn them into a book? You have all the material you need there, and you didn't even realize it was right underneath your nose. There's another book that's more of a quote book, and you can take some ideas and quotes. You might have tweets.

You might have sent out maybe 50 or 100 tweets on how to do your job better. Assemble those tips into a book, add lines in the book so people can write their own thoughts and ideas like a daily devotional, and that's book! Get away from the idea that your book has to be 300 pages long and weigh five pounds. Instead, your book could be as simple as quotes. It could be repurposed recycled material that you've already written. It can be a lot of things.

I attended a seminar a few weeks ago. The keynote presenter was a great customer service speaker. He was at the top of his game. He consults with many great companies, and he gave us copies of his (very thin) book before we entered the room.

At the end, he asked for questions. I said, "I learned a lot from your speech, and I love your book. It's very wonderful but it's also very small, only 68 pages. Is this the future of business books?" He said, "It most definitely is." I said, "How so?"

He responded, "I wrote this book for front line service professionals: people who wait on you at tables and hotel clerks, for instance. They don't want to read about the history of customer service. They don't care about the psychology of social proof. They want an easy format. I have inspiring quotes, short stories, pictures, cartoons, something that will engage and change them in 68 pages."

What is the purpose of *your* book? Format it so that it meets that purpose, and you will have written your book in a flash.

It doesn't have to be an encyclopedia. You do not need to write your book from beginning to end. Many people self-sabotage because that first chapter is very hard to write. For you, chapter five be difficult to write because it's something you don't know that much about and it scares you.

Create a deep outline. That means, for example, you have chapter four, then 10 stories (or 10 elements) within that chapter. Today, you might feel like writing about part three in chapter four, because you're inspired about that. We all have biorhythms. Some days we're more excited and more interested and some days we're less so. Follow your biorhythms and attack the parts of your outline as you see fit.

Some people are more numbers oriented. Let's say your book is 25,000 words long and you have 10 chapters. Why 10? Because that's a nice divisible number. You could always have a few more or less, but let's stick with 10 because that's easy, and everything is divisible by 10. If you have 10 chapters and want 25,000 words for the book, that's 2,500 words per chapter. You now know how long your chapter needs to be. Every chapter is 2,500 words long.

Set your pomodoro tomato clock to 15 or 30 minutes. I was a former newspaper reporter, so I can write fast. We can all write fast or run fast if we simply add a deadline.

If you say, "I'll write 1,000 words today. I'll set my timer for 30 minutes." At the end of 30 minutes, the alarm sounds and you have more energy, a few more ideas, and you finish it. It's hard to do 100 sit ups, but if you do the first one, you can do the second one, then the third, and fourth, up to 30.

That first one is always the hardest. If you play this as a numbers game, say, "I'll write 500 words a day or 1,000 words a day..." Do the math and you'll discover you can write a book in less than 90 days. Use pre-existing content including your blogs, speeches and transcripts. You can do it in a weekend. I've seen it done.

If you lack those skills, that's what ghostwriters and editors are for. Some people make tens of thousands of dollars per minute because they're selling real estate, bonds, or something in the stock market. It's not worth their time to spend 40, 50 or 100 hours writing a book.

Other people love writing and editing writing books, and will work for a very reasonable fee. The return on your investment will be outstanding. Look at the value of one client. If it's $6,000, $8,000 or $10,000, you'll make your own money back on the first or second client. You have that book forever. It's an investment in yourself.

I believe in branding. My book is "Write Your Book in a Flash." Go to WriteYourBookInAFlash.com and you'll read about my services where I can help you with coaching or editing, plus additional free resources.

You'll see a pop-up box that says, "Download a free chapter from my book on how to overcome the limiting beliefs that stop you from writing." Download that. You'll read it and think, "This exercise helped me get over that fear I had. I feel better about writing my book, so I'll hire Dan to work with me."

Let's have a conversation. If it's a good fit for us, we'll work together. If it isn't, I'll be the first person to say it isn't. If you go to Nordstrom's and buy shoes that don't fit well, they won't fit any better two weeks later.

No one wants a bad relationship, so if it looks like it will work out, I'd love to chat with you to see if we can work together. Buy my book for $2.99 on Amazon Kindle. There are techniques to write, edit, and publish your book properly, for less than $5, or $19.95 for the print copy.

I look forward to learning more about you and how I can help you write the book of your dreams, in a flash.

Next Steps

1. Do you know what the PURPOSE of your book is for readers?

2. Do you have a book coach, or have you looked into one?

3. Do you have a detailed enough outline for your book so that you can make some progress on your book every day, even if it's just grabbing quotes for each chapter?

4. Do you have beta readers to look at the first draft of your book?

5. Which method will you use to write your book in a flash: transcriptions or blog posts?

6. What is your daily writing goal, i.e. 20 minutes or 2000 words?

Dan's Contact Information

- [Write Your Book in a Flash](#) (Amazon book)

- [WriteYourBookInAFlash.com](#) (website)

Want to become a guest on the Marketer of the Day podcast?

MarketerOfTheDay.com/guest

And enter your information!

Chapter 10: Get That Consistent Stream of New Leads by Joe Kashurba

Joe Kashurba grew the freelance web design business he started in high school into a digital agency with a virtual team and clients around the world. Joe went from building $300 websites to building $30,000 websites and managing six-figure digital advertising budgets for some of the largest manufacturing and

construction companies. Joe now advises and mentors other freelance web designers and digital agency owners on how to develop and scale their businesses.

Our web design business focuses on some industrial manufacturing clients that many people don't focus on. We are also helping freelancers and agency owners grow their web design businesses and get more clients. We're taking a different approach to that. There's a lot of resources online for how to pick up a freelance client here, an agency client there, and we're helping those businesses put systems in place to get lots of clients on a consistent basis, rather than trying to do some extra grinding to pick up a client.

There are "flashy" industries and businesses. People think of innovative startups, but there are many businesses that have money and have a lot of resources in less flashy fields. If you're working with industrial, manufacturing or excavating companies you need to get them results from digital marketing and their website. In a lot of cases it's very simple compared to an industry that's flashier and doing digital marketing and has a great website.

They need the advanced techniques to get results, but you can use simple techniques to get amazing results.

Let's say you were trying to sell a $7 eBook or online course for $7. You need Facebook ads, a webinar, and ten zillion InfusionSoft funnels to get it to work. If you're an industrial company selling some chemical process or a machine shop, you run a simple Google Ads campaign with a simple landing page without a lead magnet.

It can be extremely profitable because of the high dollar nature of the services that are being offered and from the standpoint that your competitors aren't at that level of sophistication yet.

Every business needs a strategy to obtain leads and clients. Many freelancers and business owners believe clients will come to them. Somehow they'll magically grow their business. They need to take responsibility for going out and getting clients.

We've used cold emails, direct mail, and Google Ads to find web design clients. It's important to have something happening every day in the business to get more business. That can be an ad campaign running Google or Facebook Ads, sending cold emails or direct mail. Do *something* to get clients.

When I meet with a web design client (one of these industrial companies) I try to understand what they want, what they need and what's happening on their end.

Many web designers discuss what they can do with WordPress plugins. If a business owner runs a $10 million industrial company, they don't care about those details. They have specific problems and needs. That could include more requests for proposals for a specific service. We talk about what they want, and offer to help.

In that initial consultation, I identify their wants and needs. I ask why they want to meet. Usually, the answer is, "We could do a better job on the website." That's a surface level answer.

I keep digging until, for example, they admit they're not getting enough requests for proposal. I'll respond, "We want to get you more proposal requests. We want to build a high-converting website that brings in more emails, calls and people requesting proposals. I'll examine other problems and unmet needs.

We might identify forms, documents and employee resources that are needed. They might want a simple password protected members area for employees. I create a list of what they want. In the end, I tell them we can help.

Here's how we would build the website: many times, the potential client doesn't know what they want. In a consultation, we give clarity about what they want. Frequently, they'll answer with that "initial" answer: "We need a better website." They don't connect it back to wanting more leads or requests for proposals.

After meeting with us, that client has a better vision of what they want. We give them clarity. They might have met with other web designers or thought about other directions. Those other web designers discussed WordPress plugins, SEO, and XML sitemaps. Our conversation is the only one where we discussed requests for proposals, leads, and what's going on in their business.

Business owners don't care about geeky technical details. They know about their business and what's going on in their business.

I love consistent deal flow: a constant stream of new incoming leads. Proposals are constantly sent. If someone is not a good fit, choose not to work with them. Charge premium prices. Don't be afraid somebody can't afford your fee because you have constant deal flow.

When we're generating leads with Google Ads, for instance, many prospects email or call us. We'll talk for five minutes and decide they are not an ideal fit for us. I sometimes refer that lead to someone else.

I close 50 percent of in-person and serious phone consultations: some immediately and others later in the process.

There are two reasons why the closing ratio is so high. First, we ensure the "sales" component is about what that prospects wants and needs, and we offer a solution. Second, we have a "lead generation" process in place so that we speak to the right people. Often, we'll list a starting price for websites. That prospect travels through the lead generation process. They're already a good fit once we speak on the phone.

The next step after a consultation varies. Some people will be ready to go immediately. Frequently, I'll walk into a meeting and leave with a check. That prospect might have business partners or a board who needs more details.

We don't spend a lot of time writing proposals. We have templated proposals that list the essentials. It's mostly an agreement. The selling happens in that consultation and not in the proposal.

We have project managers that manage projects and help the client gather their content. When the check and signed proposal arrive, I'll send out a welcome email, which says, "Thank you for deciding to work with us." It introduces them to their assigned project manager that will work with them on the project. I'll have a conversation with that project manager. The project manager reaches out within two days about the information we still need from them, as well as the questions we have.

The design phase of the project begins: building on WordPress, custom designing in Photoshop. We show the design in Photoshop, get approval, and work with them to get the content, photos and functionality figured out.

In the development phase: we build it in WordPress. That client reviews it at the design phase, then they're working on content, reviewing the site again.

Once everything's built, it's time for the final review.

That's how the process should go. In practical realistic terms, people need changes, and there's back-and-forth. The best way to combat that is to realize that you, like any other business, have a process. People must go through that process.

Many web designers feel they must comply with every client request and add features for free. Get firm about the process: this is what we charge, and here is how it works. Let people understand they must follow that process.

The same repeat mistakes occur in many industries. Business owners (including you) need a reliable way to bring in leads. Too many web designers and freelancers rely on word of mouth or referrals as the only way to obtain new business. Because they only get one or two referrals per month, they have no choice but to comply any demand from a client, because that's the business owner's only opportunity to make money that month.

Get enough leads so you can be more selective about the clients you select. Then, increase your prices. If someone doesn't like your process, or it doesn't work out for any reason while you're halfway through a project, you can be direct and state, "This isn't a good fit." That's fine because you have consistent leads. The problems web designers and freelancers experience begin with slow lead generation: they're beholden to those few, inconsistent, precious referrals.

We run Google Ads for our web design business, but we're also still doing local and semi-local in-person meetings, which I enjoy and am good at. Some people prefer in-person meetings, others are better at phone selling.

When marketing via email, we find lists of people in a specific industry. We comb Google to locate businesses with decent websites that could be better. After creating that list, we apply our email template and get in touch.

The start of all marketing is when you know who, what and why:

- Who are you marketing to?
- What service will you offer them?
- Why? What are their needs? What are their problems?

What are the main benefits you can help with? That's the first thing we figure out. What's a target market (industry) to market to? How can you help them? What are the main things they want? Many people claim they've tried Google Ads or email and "it didn't work." These marketing strategies don't work until you figure out who you are targeting and what you offer. Then, it's all about scaling up.

Many people think they must publish blog posts and post to Facebook. You only need one solid way to find leads, then scale up. Some people are split between many lead-generation activities. If they focused one thing that was working, they'd be set.

If you're interested in our done-for-you service, where we build a website or work with your online marketing or digital marketing campaign, go to KashurbaWebDesign.com. If you're a freelancer interested in starting a freelance business, growing a web design agency, or building a digital agency, go to JoeKashurba.com.

Next Steps

1. What are you doing to contact new potential clients, i.e. Google Ads, direct mail, cold emails, phone calls?

2. Are you building lists of people or businesses in your industry to contact?

3. Are you pushing your new prospects to a consultation call?

4. On that consultation call, are you listening to their wants & needs?

5. After each meeting, do you create a custom proposal?

6. Do you plan and track the phases of work you'll do for clients? (i.e. design, development, content?)

Joe's Contact Information

- KashurbaWebDesign.com (done for you service)

- JoeKashurba.com (grow your freelance business or agency)

Chapter 11: Create a Great Customer Experience by Kenneth Bator

Ken Bator has over 15 years of experience helping organizations create environments where employees want to come to work and customers want to keep coming back.

He helps organizations align their brand, culture and strategy. In other words, Ken helps them completely understand, "What's the image we want to portray to the public? What's experience do we want to create both for and through our employees? How do we drive more of the right business to our business?"

I've worked with many solopreneurs in the past and have the distinct pleasure of attending networking groups. Some of my attendees wonder, "Does this apply to me and the size of my business?" It applies to you, especially if you're a service-based business. The experience with your client is as important, or more important, than the product you deliver.

I'm a solopreneur. I have team members, but no employees. I understand brand culture and strategy.

If you're the smartest person in the room, you're in the wrong room. You're in trouble. I'm not sure about your company size, but the experience for your customer is more important than your product. Learn how to create an experience that meets or exceeds expectations.

A concrete example: one of my favorite solopreneur clients is a therapeutic massage specialist. She rents space and works on a freelance basis with her customers. She creates a unique experience. She arrives early to an appointment to ensure specific candles, scents, and music are setup. This aligns with her brand, and her clients appreciate that she applies attention to detail, and isn't in a rush.

When she makes house calls, she doesn't use just any massage table. She uses an upgraded massage table with a special headrest and speakers. She creates a specific, consistent experience that her clients have come to love. This helps her sustain AND grow her business.

Write and implement service standards. If you're a solopreneur or you have a team of 5 or 500, write down specific standards. Example: "I will arrive 15 minutes early for my client appointment. Greet the customer when he or she walks through the door within five seconds."

Those written instructions become ingrained in your mind, and you don't have to guess if you setup your table a certain way, or if you should arrive at your bank teller job on time or 10 minutes early. You can follow this every single day.

That way of thinking improves the experience become better. Plus, making decisions ahead of time removes decisions. You follow a checklist. Online, this still applies. You most likely use the same membership software, service for taking payments, and landing page software.

It's a win-win. This provides a better experience for new customers, and we know what we're doing. That masseuse gets repeat customers. People come back because they know what to expect.

When you have a consistent way to engage people, life becomes easier. I work with many financial institution clients. Take a financial advisor, for example. If you're working for a large firm, you're still, in a way, running your own solopreneur business. One service standard that many of my clients adopt is, "I will answer all calls and emails within three hours." Apply that standard to a current client email or Facebook message referral, you have that consistent level of a service standard. That individual will say, "I engaged or reached out to this person online, and 89 minutes later, I have a return message."

I don't trust some marketers or companies. I'm uncertain if I should buy. I'm not sure if the payment will work, or if they will discount the price later. I like other marketers quite a bit. I think to myself, I trust buying from this company because I know they'll respond to any issue I might have. Service standards.

How do you decide if you're doing too much? Replying within three hours is a great way of going the extra mile. Are there times when that commitment gets in the way of being productive?

If you put a service standard on paper, have the resources and wherewithal to adhere to it. For some people, three hours could be unrealistic. 24 hours or 48 hours could be a better fit. If it creates an issue with efficiency or consistency in your service, don't write it down or change it.

If you are fortunate enough to already have service standards and haven't reviewed them, take the time to review them, by yourself, or toss it to your team. There could be an operational reason for you being unable to respond in three hours. It could be five hours, or you could change the service standard to implement an automated response in three minutes.

If this creates an issue with productivity, take a hard look at the service standard, or change it for the betterment of the business. It isn't set in stone. You can review and change it up.

There's a credit union in the Midwest. Fortunately, they have a great culture. I advised them to add this service standard: to work with any given customer on a first name basis. This allowed us to create a consistent message and brand a certain way. We added family-oriented pictures when posting on Facebook. When we send emails, we concentrate on what we do naturally, working with people on a first name basis, rather than using stock copy or wording, and that has helped a great deal.

Their income is increasing. Their membership is up about 10%. It's not only about grabbing another customer, member or client. It's about engaging for better profitability and getting good service.

To begin the process, I take the management or the owner down a line of questioning that begins with one or two simple questions:

Question #1: Who do you want to serve?

Question #2: What problem do you want to solve? Once you know what niche you'd like to serve and what problem you'd like to solve, messaging and service standards are much easier.

That massage therapist client understood what it was like to be a pregnant woman, and had specific programs to help other pregnant women. We knew exactly who we wanted to serve, so that when she applied her email marketing, she spoke specifically to the problems pregnant women have, and how her massage service helped alleviate those problems.

People don't buy products and services. They buy solutions to their problems.

Who do you want to serve and what problem do you solve? It's rare that I'll outright tell a client what their problem is, or what they should do. I take them down a path of discovery and it becomes part of them. It's their idea, essence, and image in their mind. Going through the steps of helping them grow their business based on that idea becomes easier.

I'm rarely the smartest guy in the room. Any solopreneur, entrepreneur, or business owner, should know their business better than I ever will. My talent is not telling them what they should do, but being able to see the situation from a fresh perspective. Many times, the business owner or solopreneur knows the answer to the question of how to grow. They simply need help coming to the solution themselves.

The biggest solopreneurial problem is focus. There are many legitimate make money opportunities, but many consumers need help. When you have an entrepreneurial mind and personality, you have a habit of shifting from idea to idea. "Less is more" makes sense.

During the Great Recession, consulting clients and speaking gigs weren't falling off the tree like they once were. I added a couple services. I began processing credit cards for small businesses and selling loyalty programs to them. This scattered my business so much that not only did the main core of consulting and speaking suffer, it damaged my brand. Some small businesses knew me as the credit card guy, others as the loyalty program guy. I only offered those services.

These days, I'm the brand, culture and strategy alignment guy. It took a while to eliminate those service offerings to bring my brand messaging back in line to make people realize what I offered. This is my focus for you.

The next step: go to my website at BTCInc.net. The homepage has a button that says, "If your formula doesn't add up, click here." Clicking that button gives you a free whitepaper teaching you branding, culture and strategy alignment. It gives straightforward tips that a solopreneur, entrepreneur, or a business owner can implement immediately to improve your brand, culture, and strategy.

Next Steps

1. Do you know what problem your business solves? What is it?

2. What service standard, i.e. showing up early, replying to email within 3 hours, can you commit to?

3. Which service standards do you already have in place that you can review?

Ken's Contact Information

- BTCInc.net (Bator Branding and Consulting)

Chapter 12: Goals, Finances, Budgeting & Growth by Ruby Tan

Ruby Tan from CelaBookkeeping.com provides bookkeeping services to her clients. However, she realized that many businesses have run into financial problems. Many of them are surviving from paycheck to paycheck, and without the next check, there's no way to pay the bills. She's involved with Mike Michalowicz's Profit First and has a mission to eradicate entrepreneur poverty.

I was born in Indonesia and grew up in Malaysia, then came to the US for further study. I married and had children, and my husband lost his job in early 2000. I wasn't making much at that time, so we lost the breadwinner. We had a mortgage and bills to pay. We did not have a lot of other credit card debt, but we still had debt in terms of a mortgage. I love budgeting. I like to handle, work out, play around with finances and numbers. I prepared a 5-and 7-year budget.

Not only did we get out of the situation, my husband went back to school, finished and got a different type of job, totally different from what he was doing. Also, we were able to pay off our mortgage within that seven-year period. I said, "*We* can do it. I'm sure I'm able to help other families to do it," not knowing how I should do it. When I discovered *Profit First*, I became interested. I was sold immediately, and that's how I got involved with them. I now help small businesses work out their budgets. Doing a budget on paper is one thing, but practicing it is another. There is human behavior involved, and that code is very hard to crack.

During our difficult financial period, my family was in survival mode. We recognized items that were necessities versus luxuries.

Consider "that" item in your (personal or business) budget: do you NEED it or simply WANT it? You THINK you need everything, but you do not NEED everything. Our cell phone was pay-as-you-go, $100 for one year. We ate out only on birthdays. We changed our lifestyle, including shopping at different stores. We scrutinized every single penny going out.

We continued using credit cards to collect miles. Within that seven-year period, we visited Malaysia using free tickets. We have been frugal in our spending. My husband is a deal seeker. We find credit card deals with bonus mile offers and take advantage of them. When you find a deal like that, don't settle for the first one you find: look for the second or third, at least.

We changed our spending habits. At one point, a friend reminded me to be faithful in my tithing. Our income had been slashed 70%, but when I returned to work, we were faithful in our tithing, and the blessing was tremendous. Not just financially, but we had good health. My cherry tree produced so much. The prior year, it produced only six cherries. The year when my husband was laid off, it produced 60 pounds. The next year, 80 pounds. We had so much in abundance, we gave them away.

Tithing was 10%, included in the budget. If I had not included that in the budget, we would never have been able to find the money for it. Once we ended our "rough patch", I finished my degree without any student loan. Our house was paid off, so I was able to return to school, earn my bachelor's degree and open my own bookkeeping service, which I've been running since 2013.

My college-aged son has learned to budget. God willing, he will graduate without any debt.

We didn't start with a master plan. One thing led to another, and when we paid off our house, we could use the money for other things. I returned to school because I didn't have that monthly payment anymore. We have to pay taxes, but we set that money aside. We homeschooled our boys at first, until we were able to send them to a Christian high school to help them grow spiritually and physically.

You cannot imagine the freedom you'll experience once you get out of debt!

Many people don't realize what they're spending because charges are deducted from checking or credit card accounts. That's one problem.

Avoid buying too many things you don't need. With Profit First methodology, we work with clients to see where they stand. We divide expenses, taxes, anything set aside, and look at the percentages.

With Profit First, when you deposit $10,000 worth of sales, you do not spend that $10,000 because you will move the $10,000 to different places. For example, owners pay the profit account, taxes account, an operating account, and so on. What you could spend out of that $10,000 is only $3,000 because you have other obligations.

You must pay your vendors, taxes, employees, and ensure you get paid. That's why Profit First works well for entrepreneurs. Many people have success stories, including me.

Before I joined Profit First, I volunteered with Crown Ministries' money life coaching, coaching individuals and families struggling with debt on a personal level. I have helped to slash personal expenses.

Now I'm doing it for businesses. It's somewhat similar. Business owners may find help hard to accept and feel it's unneeded. A common mistake is that a purchase is "tax deductible." True, it may be tax deductible or regular expenses. Whether or not it's necessary is another matter. Vendors will tell you, "Don't worry. It's tax deductible." Very sad. I would rather have the money to spend than to deduct the taxes.

If you're tired of being broke month after month, have the courage to say, "I'm tired and need to change."

If you're willing to learn, you can. Previously, my husband and I never thought of paying off our mortgage early. Sometimes we are forced into circumstances to help us make wiser decisions later.

We're focusing on helping more individuals reach their personal or business goals. You cannot change the past, but you can proceed in a new direction for the future.

I provide bookkeeping services, but I don't file taxes. I provide "Profit First" consultations and coaching, relating to finances.

To learn more about my services, visit my website at celabookkeeping.com or call me on the phone at 630-768-2558.

Set aside money. Prepare the umbrella before it rains.

Next Steps

1. Do you have a budget for your finances, so you track money coming in and out?

2. Which wasteful expenses will you commit to removing from your spending?

3. What exceptions will you make to those rules, i.e. going out to eat for birthdays, or tithing?

4. What percentage of profits will you commit to set aside?

5. If you are struggling with your finances, who can you contact to get advice?

Ruby's Contact Information

- CelaBookkeeping.com (bookkeeping services)

- Phone: 630-768-2558

Chapter 13: Create, Qualify and Close Phone Leads by Glen Shelton

Glen Shelton is the founder of LeadHeroes.com. In early 2015, he realized there had to be a better way to obtain tele-marketed leads. As an independent agent, he's tried all types of lead sources from live telemarketer avatars, voicemail, direct mail, and the internet. He realized the leads with the highest return-on-investment (as well as being high in quality) were live telemarketer leads.

The telephone has existed for 150 years, but it's still crucial to the sales process. Depending on the service or product you're looking to sell (especially something higher end), a phone call needs to happen to land that sale.

My background is specific to insurance, where many times, you call someone on the phone, for a conversation or to set an appointment. Some people don't need the phone to sell dropshipping products, for example. Plenty of times, someone still needs to get on the phone. This can be entry-level grunt-work, which you shouldn't bog yourself down with if you're looking to scale your company or grow your profits as a salesperson.

Setting up a call center is a lot of work. Some people dabble and give it up. I was a full-time producing insurance agent, and I had to stop producing from insurance sales because it was so much work to manage my call center, to hire and scale.

People ask me, "Why would I pay you when I could do this myself for a lower price?" They'll cite prices. It can be done for less, but it's a time game. I sell time.

I help you to offload low-level time-wasting tasks. I'll manage that process for you, so you can focus on high-level moneymaking activities that increase your bottom-line and upline.

I built the foundation of my company by cold calling for lead generation. We've experimented to grow, use different methods, and explore new verticals. We set appointments from our internal database or a list you provide us. We can accept contact data, or leads submitted online -- called direct mail leads. Anything phone related. We can take inbound calls. There are many opportunities.

My business is a Swiss army knife. Many things are possible with a call center: an answering service, customer service, outbound, scheduling, appointment setting. My background is insurance, specifically, the senior insurance market, but it could cross into any vertical.

We're successful because we go straight to the source. I spent several weeks in the Philippines networking, exploring, learning the culture, meeting with my existing employees, looking for new employees. There's no middleman.

If you're looking to use a call center, regardless of who you work with, go to the source. There are many middlemen in the marketing game. I'll see people reselling someone else's services. I've looked at large companies who outsource call centers overseas, for example, Chase Bank. I called and was immediately talking to an operator overseas. Large companies have been leveraging this for years: outsourced work overseas for lower labor costs.

I can bring that to small and medium sized businesses. I work with 100% individual independent agents who don't have a large staff or an office. They might be working out of their home. You don't need to be a large company to do work with me or to find a call center.

Your marketing budget doesn't need to be massive, but you can't show up with 50 dollars and expect that to take you to the moon. There are expenses and a ramp-up period as you figure out what does and does not work. Adjust to this new marketing style if you're not used to using a call center for your marketing. This applies to individuals, small businesses and medium businesses.

Many people want to sample, and I'm all about that. I have minimums as low as $250 to run a campaign. However, sometimes, the sample size is too small to get an accurate short- or long-term representation. That's the battle I fight.

Those clients within my customer base who order larger quantities, pay for more leads, and have a bigger marketing budget are significantly happier. I can accommodate people with a smaller budget, at least at first. The correct way of approaching this is to have a budget in place and track it over four to twelve weeks, then view results at the end to determine what's working and what can be improved. We continue to tweak or move on to something else.

If someone wants to work with us, we have different verticals. We've made calls for real estate which is different from our insurance verticals. A good-sized budget is $1,000 to $2,000. How quickly you rinse and repeat that budget is up to you, your business, and the conversion on our call center marketing. That's a good-sized budget where you can get enough quantity. Some services cost more because it takes us more time, the data we use is higher quality, or comes from a different source. Ideally, $1,000 and higher gives you a good sample size.

Once we decide to work together, we come up with a plan. If it's a new vertical or a script we haven't tried, there can be back-and-forth, learning, tweaking. I feel like an experimenting mad scientist, which is what marketing comes down to: A/B split testing. It's used in marketing software, books, and online. It's the same in the call center environment. Changing one single word can make a huge difference. Recently we changed the phrase "Call Back" to "Contact Us" and it's having a positive effect for us and the clients we work with. You must test. If me and my team are working with a new script or a new vertical, it takes time and testing to figure it out.

STANDARD	REAL-TIME	LIVE TRANSFER	PRE-SET APPOINTMENT
Ages: 55 - 80 | Income Range: 0 - 50K	Ages: 55 - 80 | Income Range: 0 - 50K	Ages: 55 - 80 | Income Range: 0 - 50K	Ages: 55 - 80 | Income Range: 0 - 50K
Leads targeting Seniors who may have failed to save for the inevitable funeral costs that their family will incur in the event of their passing. We batch these leads out at the end of every night, completed orders delivered in 5 business days or less.	We took our standard FE lead script, added a health qualifying question, and send the lead immediately via text, email or CRM. No more waiting, receive leads in real time as we generate them!	Designed for call centers or agencies of 5 or agents. Qualified for interest, health and warm transferred instantly! Eliminate any wasted time trying to chase leads who won't answer their phone.	Tired of managing an appointment setter? Look no further! We dialed in our personalized pre-set appointment program to save you time and keep you focused on selling. Most agents have reported a sit ratio of 70% or better!
▶ Sample 1	▶ Sample 1	▶ Sample 1	▶ Sample 1
▶ Sample 2	▶ Sample 2	▶ Sample 2	▶ Sample 2
Script	Script	Script	Script
BUY	BUY	BUY	BUY

At LeadHeroes.com, on the insurance leads page, we show our samples and scripts. It's all fixed price. You don't need to setup an account, it's pay-as-you-go, and we don't auto-bill you like others do. If you're consultant or you're in a different vertical from what we're already doing, that's more of an experimental run. We'll talk about the area, target demographic, script you want to use, goals for the campaign, and your marketing.

There are many variables. Some clients or prospects want a simple black-and-white answer... "What's the closing percentage?" Or, "How many people can you call in this area?" There are different times of day to make phone calls. Some areas are better. Rural areas (secondary markets) perform very well across all marketing and advertising platforms since primary markets get saturated quickly.

If Lead Heroes is already in that vertical and having success, it's plug-and-play. Not much needs to happen. If you operate in a niche we are not in, it's more of a consultation phone call to decide if we're a good fit.

I closely watch the numbers of a particular long-standing client to ensure it stays viable. I'm curious if a closing percentage drops, an area is bad, or one of my team members is under-performing. In that sense, in the insurance vertical, I have the data.

The senior market answers the phone and are receptive to it, so most of what we do targets the senior market. These people have home phones, answer the phone, and are excited to speak with someone. If you're a senior living in a rural area, you're likely to answer that phone and share information with us. Typically, it's a brief phone call to gather information to pass along to a sales expert.

People aged 20 to 40 don't have home phones. Most aren't talking on the phone nearly as much as the older crowd. That's where inbound or customer service solutions would be more effective. Appointment scheduling could work best for you, customer service, inbound phone calls, confirmations for delivery or products. I get that question, "Glenn, cold calling will die or call centers will disappear." I answer, "Yes and no." Like I said earlier, the phone has been around for 150 plus years. It's not going anywhere any time soon. It will continue to change and evolve, but we still need to talk. That's how we communicate. We must speak with people.

We haven't yet done media buying and scheduling speaking engagements. If you have an idea that applies outside our fixed price offers, we come up with a custom rate. If we have enough activity in that niche or vertical, we offer a fixed price service. Out of the gate, we can't promise a fixed price or specific results without the experimentation phase.

We've dabbled in B2B and could do lot more in that space. Seminars are red hot. I'd love to get involved in that invitation space. I've done seminars as an insurance agent previously myself. I wish I had had a call center behind me so we could have had more people show up in that seminar. It doesn't have to be cold calling. The majority of what we do is cold calling, but it can also be: inbound, warm leads, people who found you on your website, etc.

There are numerous variables to any job. We can make 10,000 to 15,000 phone calls on a $2,000 budget.

This is high volume and high speed. That's what separates us from smaller companies where one person makes calls. We make a lot of calls in a short amount of time. I'm able to manage the quality from start to finish and that's what sets us apart. What do you think you could do with 10,000 to 15,000 phone calls?

The power of a call center and being able to reach out to that many people that quickly with human interaction is what we've been doing for thousands of years.

If you're an entrepreneur, an independent sales rep, or you're looking to do something different, structure your finances as a business would, even if you aren't technically incorporated. Don't look at marketing as something that costs money. Look at it as the life blood of your business. Realize you want to allocate as much money as you can to marketing.

When it comes to ROI, you can't only look at a single week. Look at 30 to 90 days of results. It takes follow-up depending on the service platform and vertical, and what you're hoping to accomplish. Many times, comparing lead generation from 7 days versus 90 days, there could be a five times difference in closing percentage. We handle the marketing, and anything call center related for you. When it comes to sales, do it yourself or have someone who sells those leads for you.

Next Steps

1. What is one low-level time wasting task you can outsource in your business?

2. Which call center method sounds best for you and your business, i.e. appointment scheduling, inbound calls, or cold calling?

3. What size budget can you dedicate to pay a call center?

4. What is your ultimate goal (i.e. less refunds, more sales, more clients) with call center marketing?

Glen's Contact Information

To implement call center marketing in your business, visit LeadHeroes.com. Go to the "Contact Us" page and submit a message or schedule a phone call.

Chapter 14: Make Money Using Raw Land by Mark Podolsky

Mark Podolsky, The Land Geek, is considered the country's foremost authority on buying and selling raw undeveloped land within the United States. He's been actively investing in real estate and raw land since 2001 and has completed 5000+ unique transactions. He's the host of one of the top-rated podcasts in the investing category on iTunes, "The Best Passive Income Model"

and *"The Art of Passive Income."* He's also the host of the Land Geek podcast.

If you're at all interested in unconventional real estate, or you've heard about raw land, allow me to jump right in and present a fun scenario for you. Let's pretend I visit a county in Texas and obtain their tax delinquent list. I notice that someone (who lives in California) owes $200 in back taxes. This tells me that Californian has no emotional attachment to that land and no longer values it because they are late on their taxes. They could be financially distressed.

I'll examine the comparable sales for the last 12 to 18 months and divide by four. That number is what Warren Buffet calls a 300% margin of safety. I'll send you, the Californian, an offer for that property. Let's say that property in Texas has a comp of $10,000. The most I will offer you is $2,500. Three to five percent of people will accept this "top dollar offer" because they've been getting notices every month and eventually they'll lose this property, either in a tax deed or a tax lien auction. They think, $2,500 is better than nothing, and they accept your offer.

I perform due diligence, a fancy word for research. Does this person own the property? Are the taxes $200 or $2,000? Is there legal access to the property? Are there liens or encumbrances on the property? Is the title free and clear? I have a checklist with these questions. If everything looks okay, I buy the property. I now own it for $2,500 and already have built-in buyers: the neighbors! I send out neighbor letters saying, "If you want to expand your holdings or protect your view before I take this to the open market, I'm giving you the first right to buy this property at $10,000."

A percentage of those people buy them. If they pass, I'll go to my buyer's list. If the buyer's list passes, I'll visit Craigslist and use special software that posts 128 ads in one click. If that doesn't work, I'll visit Facebook Buy/Sell groups. My last resort is to visit eBay to liquidate.

I sell that property within 30 days. I'll sell it for $2,500 down and $449 per month, about the same as a car payment. This gets my capital out within the down payment or within six months of the down payment. In this scenario, I've created a $449 per month passive income stream for the next 5 to 10 years at 9% interest with no renters, no rehabs, no renovations, no rodents. I'm not dealing with a tenant, so I'm exempt from Dodd-Frank, RESPA and the Safe Act. There is no owner's real estate legislation.

I continue this process until I create enough passive income on these land notes so that it exceeds my fixed expenses. I'm now working because I want to, not because I have to. Also, we've automated 90% of the business with software. I work 2 hours a week in frontier properties. It's automated and scalable.

Many people are moving the needle in their lives by doing this model. Shawn and Rachel Rickman created $4,500 in monthly passive income last year, quit their jobs and are running their land business with their laptops while traveling through Europe. They keep doing deals and traveling because they can do it from anywhere in the world. It's these types of stories that motivate me every day to keep teaching and keep getting better at what I do. We shuffle paper and we make money.

It wasn't always this way for me. I used to be a very miserable investment banker and I specialized in mergers and acquisitions with private equity groups. Mid-market, 5 to 500 million in enterprise value, and I hated it. I had a 45-minute commute to work and back, I was micromanaged, I had long pressure filled hours. Very stressful, no control. It got so bad, that I wouldn't get the Sunday blues anticipating Monday rolling around, I'd get the Friday blues anticipating the weekend going by quickly and having to be back at work on Monday.

My firm hired someone who goes to tax deed auctions. For $2,000, he buys property for pennies on the dollar, flips it online and makes on average a 300% return on his investment. I look at companies all day long. A great company has 15% margins or free cash flow. An average company is at 10% and I'm looking at companies all day long less than 10% so I don't believe that he's making 300%.

I had $3,000 saved up for car repairs. I went to New Mexico with him and did exactly what he said. I bought 10 half-acre parcels in New Mexico at an average price of $300 each, put them online that next week, and they all sold for an average price of over $1200. 300 percent. He was right. I took all that money and went to another auction in southern Arizona. No one was in the room. I bought properties left and right. After that auction, I made over $90,000 just flipping property.

I told my pregnant wife I was quitting my job to sell land full time. She said, "Absolutely not." I invested in raw land part time for 18 months until the land investing income exceeded my investment banking income. I quit my job in 2001 and have been doing this full time ever since.

These are low-ticket transactions. We're not trying to buy property in Manhattan or compete with billionaires buying up farm land to make eight percent. We're looking at distressed property maybe two to three hours from the nearest city in areas of the country like California, Florida, Nevada, Colorado, Texas, Arizona. "Fast growing" country, the sunshine states. Buying properties for 20-25 cents on the dollar. There's so much land in this country. We might spend $500 to $20,000 on a parcel. It's not big money.

I started with $3,000. My buddy Dran, who is a multimillionaire now, started with $800. Some of my clients have no money. They just lock up the property, send out neighbor letters, do a dual close. They get infinite Return-On-Investment because the neighbor buys it. It's a noncompetitive niche because HGTV is not running reality shows called "Flip This Land." That would be boring. It's me in front of my computer.

The model is simple, but it's not easy. There's also fear of the unknown. Embrace the suck with any new endeavor. That's scary and hard if you've never bought or marketed a piece of real estate. There are steps involved, and it's easier to watch the latest Netflix show and continue on with your life.

We offer tons of free information. We have a course called Flight School which is a group coaching course where you have to execute real time. If we give you a course, it's hard to execute on your own. In this way it's like personal training. Execute with your flight school class and you send out offers the first week, do due diligence the second week. There's Q&A in this 16-week program. We take you up the land investing mountain quickly, safely and efficiently so you don't get hurt. It's a 16-week timetable, but it moves fast. By week 10, you should have your first deal. You should get a 10x return on your investment on the education aspect. We take you through every step of the business step by step from getting a list and then scrubbing that list, pricing that list, sending out your offers, using our software called LGPASS, the Land Geek Proprietary Automated Software System. Automate from day one. Send the offers, they come back, you learn how to do your due diligence, we give you that checklist and then we teach you how to close quickly, efficiently, and safely with that seller. You now own that property. We provide you with that neighbor letter, and you begin mailing neighbor letters. We show you step by step how to find that list of neighbors and how to automatically send those out.

We show you how to build a buyers list, how to create a website and squeeze page, an ethical bribe and an auditor's binder series, and you go step by step by step until you start selling your property and then we automate it on the back end.

We have a program called GeekPay.io that automates the collection of the note payments every single month with notifications via ACH. You're insured, you'll get paid and we take you through it every step of the way. There's a question and answer period and you're not alone. You're guided and you must do it.

You're in a class, there's accountability, and you get a different feel than slogging through a textbook.

The only thing you own is your list of potential land investors. Facebook could change their algorithm and not allow it. Craigslist could change their algorithm and not allow it. If you can build a list of people that know and trust you, send them a promotion every week to buy raw land. Build that over time so you're not dependent on any platforms to sell property.

The list is built from people that are interested in buying raw land or have previously bought raw land from you.

Good artists copy, great artists steal. I tell people to take my bribe. Know how to avoid the three fatal land buying mistakes. Teach and educate your potential customer how to be a better land investor. That builds trust and credibility. When they are ready to pull that trigger, they know you have their back. You've taught them how to be a better land investor.

Three to five percent of people accept your offer. If that number is under three percent, you've offered too little for that property. If it's over five percent, you've probably gone too high and need to re-trade. Those are the metrics that follow your mailings.

People tend to either love marketing or love deal flow. Engineering types love deal flow and analysis. Creative types love marketing: creating headlines, pictures, maps, and calls-to-action.

Making money from this business model is based on those two things: mailing and marketing. We bridge the gap between analytical and creative. Creative people can become more analytical: understand metrics, create systems and automate. Those people that are analytical need help avoiding paralysis-by-analysis. They can become more creative with marketing and selling.

Creativity includes doing county research. Where would I buy this property? Find hidden gems. I get a thrill every time we make a sale and create that new relationship. We'll be living with that person for the next 5 to 30 years. Creating gifts, giving an unexpected extra to our customers. Little touches with technology and video, ways to create a more personal bond with that customer is super creative.

Due diligence can be fun. Is there a stream or a mountain on that land? How do I create more demand for that property that may not be immediately obvious?

I bought a 40-acre parcel in New Mexico for $2,500 and messed up my due diligence. Half the land, thirty inaccessible acres, was located on a mountain. Only ten acres were usable. I listed the property on eBay. I wanted out. It was a 10-day 1-dollar auction. The first day, the bidding rose to $2,500. By day 10, the winner of the auction was set to pay $32,500. I was worried, called the buyer, and said, "You won the auction, but I want to confirm you read the ad. 30 acres are not buildable, you can't do anything on it, it's just a mountain."

His response? "It's perfect. I'm a movie director in Los Angeles. I was going to travel there, and I didn't want to deal with permits. Now I can film on my own 40 acres of raw land. I need these views." Perfect! He wired the funds. The saying goes, "There's a pig for every barn."

Even if you bought swamp land, someone can grow shiitake mushrooms on that land. A client of mine, Scott Todd, bought a mud pit and profited $15,000. The buyer loved it and drove his ATV on that land, for fun.

For more information, go to TheLandGeek.com. Schedule a call with one of our Land Geek coaches and they'll walk you through it. Email support@thelandgeek.com and use the subject line "Robert Plank." We'll our $97 passive income launch kit for free. We explain how to buy and sell raw land, including deal flow, due diligence, and selling the property.

Next Steps

1. If raw land interests you, what budget do you have set aside for your first deal?

2. Which states in the U.S. interest you the most when it comes to buying raw land, i.e. California?

3. Do you prefer attending tax lien auctions or sending offer letters in the mail?

Mark's Contact Information

- TheLandGeek.com (how to invest in real estate with no money)

- GeekPay.io (collect loan payments)

- Email: support@thelandgeek.com

We are looking forward to reading your honest review at:

MarketerOfTheDay.com/amazon

See you there!

Chapter 15: Done For You Product Launches, Lead Capture & Conversion by Larry Becht

Larry Becht is a digital marketing expert who helps businesses grow exponentially by providing innovative and leading-edge direct response sales and marketing solutions. He's a ClickFunnels Certified Partner (one of only 30 in the world) and is certified

through DigitalMarketer. His company, Authority Marketing Experts, designs highly-optimized sales and marketing funnel systems paired with engaging advertising to help businesses share their message with their ideal target audience. They provide solutions for lead generation, sales, product launches, webinars, membership sites, and other strategies to help you become the authority in your area.

Business owners looking to grow their business online can do that in a few ways. We create custom opt-in funnels, sales funnels, membership sites, webinars, product launch funnels, and more. We discover what they're looking to accomplish and design the best strategy to meet those goals.

Technology and marketing concepts have changed over the years. Direct response marketing is still the most effective method and that's what we utilize. Mass market advertising (TV, Radio, Billboards, etc.) is fine if you have an unlimited budget and a big-name brand. If not, direct response marketing is a better approach. It is much more focused on identifying your ideal target markets and your right audience as the match for your product or service. We can then architect the best solution for what you're looking to do to expand your business online.

Some people begin their conversation with us by saying, "I need a Sales Funnel to sell my product or service." When we ask questions to find out more about their goals, we can then design an overall strategy that not only will effectively sell their product or service, but also help them to become an authority in their market.

One of our core platforms is ClickFunnels. I was one of the early adopters when it was first offered to the public in 2014. I was also one of the first who completed the Certified Partner Program in early 2015. Combining the capabilities of that platform with DigitalMarketer strategies provides a wide variety of solutions to quickly bring products to market.

We've used many products over the years, and ClickFunnels is our favorite. InfusionSoft (now known as Keap) is one of the largest products and they're established. However, for many people (business owners especially), it's too large, difficult, and complicated to configure and to use. ClickFunnels is the simplest solution we've seen in a long time that's still as powerful as InfusionSoft.

ClickFunnels has several components including Actionetics for a CRM (Customer Relationship Management system) and email follow-up campaigns. It has Backpack which allows affiliates to promote your product or service.

ClickFunnels integrates with payment processing systems including PayPal, Stripe, and many others. Zapier integrations means you can integrate ClickFunnels to virtually any other system or platform.

If you have a CRM in place within your business, you don't have to discard that. Import your data into Actionetics, or continue to use your existing CRM in conjunction with ClickFunnels. We have clients who use AWeber, MailChimp or ActiveCampaign and want to continue using them. They save money migrating the data from these platforms into ClickFunnels, then they shut down those other services.

One of our largest client bases is in the dental niche. We work with many dental offices across the US and Canada to help market their high-end procedures: Implants, Ortho and Cosmetic. We've developed a unique program combining compelling advertising using a variety of platforms, high-converting funnel processes, and engaging email follow-up campaigns. We help them not only attract patients for these high-end procedures, but we also help them to be recognized as the authority in their market for these treatments.

Most people realize how easy it is to attract leads for free lead magnet items, but they think it's impossible to sell high-ticket items. We've helped clients to promote low-priced products such as "free plus shipping" book funnels in the $7 range, up to $25,000 and higher products and services. The same concepts can be applied regardless of the price point.

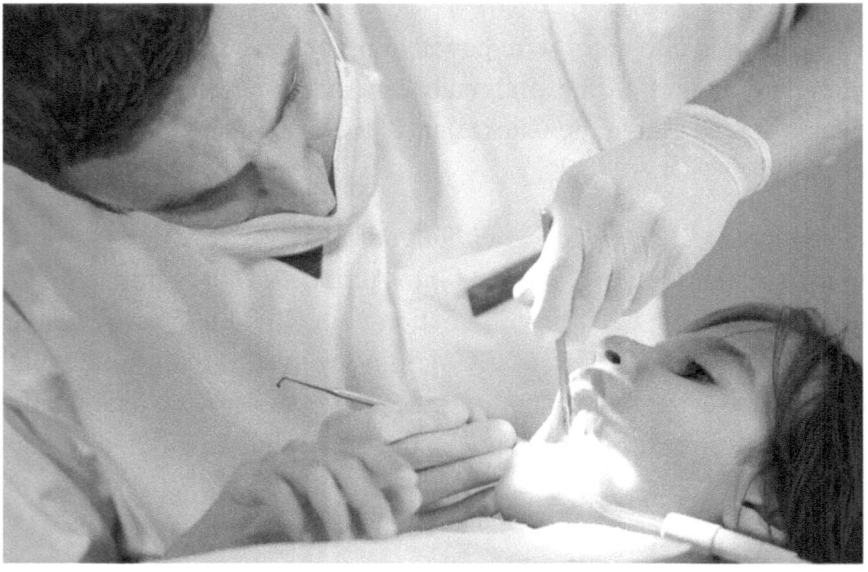

We have another dental client that has not only a hugely successful dental practice with more than ten locations but is also a coach to many other dentists around the world. We've developed countless funnel processes for this client, including webinars, membership sites, live events, mastermind groups, and sales funnels. These systems have helped him launch two multi-million dollar businesses in addition to his core dental business.

The best way to get started with us is to have a 30-minute Expert Business Explosion Strategy Session. We learn so many things by starting with the basic questions: "What's your business? What's your product or service? How are you looking to promote it?" We see where we can make recommendations and give advice.

At some point during the initial call, most business owners say, "We want to work with you. You gave me five more ideas I didn't think about. How can we get started?" That's a great way to build the relationship: finding out about their business and goals.

We have USA and international clients. The interesting change in business over the past several years is that we can work with clients around the world as easily as we can locally. Through video conferencing technologies such as Skype or Zoom, we can talk virtually face to face at any time.

Many clients call us after purchasing ClickFunnels. We often hear this: "I bought ClickFunnels and I'm in my two-week free trial. I realized it's more involved than I thought. I need to focus on my business instead of creating funnels. It's not as easy as the sales videos made it seem. We need your help."

Whether you're in your ClickFunnels two-week trial, you've heard about ClickFunnels and want to try it out, or you know there's a better way to build your web presence, have a quick chat with our team first. We can save you time because if you were to implement, that might take months. We can usually do it in days or weeks.

You might think you're saving money by not hiring experts. However, if your process isn't properly designed and takes three months to launch, you've lost thousands of dollars on potential sales and taken focus away from your business. Save yourself time and money. Hire experts like us who know exactly what to do.

For more information, and to register for a free Business Explosion Strategy Session, visit AuthorityMarketingExperts.com/Start.

Next Steps

1. Do you have a website? Does a funnel and ClickFunnels interest you?

2. Do you have a strategy to build your list and attract clients, i.e. free plus shipping book or low ticket infoproduct?

3. When will you schedule your 30-minute strategy session with Larry?

Larry's Contact Information

- AuthorityMarketingExperts.com

- AuthorityMarketingExperts.com/Start

- 719-239-3000

Chapter 16: Task and Project Management Using Asana, PipeDrive & Slack by Paul Minors

Would you like to be more organized? Have you heard of tools such as Asana, MailChimp, Pipedrive, and Zapier? Have you heard of these tools but became overwhelmed with what you had to learn? In that case, you need Paul Minors, a virtual consultant who helps businesses setup tools including Asana, MailChimp,

Pipedrive and Zapier. He's helped over 200 one-on-one clients to create more productive businesses by using the best productivity and sales tools.

There's always resistance when people use new tools. Our typical client is a business owner or company director, who has discovered a productivity tool and decided to implement it in their organization. For example, they decided Asana can help with task management, but are unsure how to use it. They need an expert to tell them what to do, set it up, and train their team.

In a larger team, some employees are less tech savvy and are resistant to change. They prefer the current status quo and ask, "Why do we need to change?" The answer: these tools are designed to make you more productive. We don't want any tool to slow you down, and if that's the case, we might need to re-examine how you're using it, along with the principles that come with it.

When rolling out a new tool (i.e. Asana, Slack, or Google Drive) to your team, a common mistake is to dump that tool on team members and expect them to use it.

That lacks a formal rollout plan. It lacks guidelines saying, "This is how we'll use it. This is how I expect you to use it. This is the way I want you to use it."

There's no introduction to the tool. Some people love it, some hate it. Everyone uses it in a different way. The team doesn't gel until you assemble everyone and agree on how that tool should be used.

Regardless of the software you're implementing, take a strategic approach to:

- how you'll roll it out to your organization
- where this tool fits in
- how people will adopt it

Asana is a task and project management tool. It began as a possible replacement for email. It was founded by Justin Rosenstein (an ex-Google employee) and Dustin Moskovitz (a co-founder of Facebook).

Scenario: You're setting up projects and laying out the scope of work. It's easier to communicate that in Asana and comment on tasks, similar to commenting on posts on Facebook. Teams don't send email (or Slack messages) to communicate internally. Communication goes through Asana.

Reason: your conversations are linked to your tasks -- your units of work.

Asana wants to be the complete ecosystem where you live and work. They want to be a full-fledged product management resource allocation tool. You can see and manage the complete hierarchy of your business, manage your visions, missions, and how projects flow into that.

It's the perfect tool to see *who* is doing *what* and by *when*. Who, what, and when. The transparency and accountability from this results in a massive increase in productivity. There is no hiding. No one on your team can say, "I didn't get your email" -- or, "I didn't have time to complete this task." Everyone can see everyone else's workload. It brings teams together and gets everyone working towards a common goal.

My business is a two-person team consisting of my wife and myself. We sit across from each other but are away from each other during the day. It's also important that we track our decisions and not rely on the messiness of email.

If Hailey needs to assign a task to me, she can send a request into Asana, and likewise, I can send a request to Hailey. We can communicate about the progress of our work or discuss decisions we've made regarding that task. Our communication is always tied to the work.

Email is not a clear mode of communication: you can have a back-and-forth conversation all day, and are still confused about who's doing what and when.

A task in Asana can say, "Complete this weekly report. It's assigned to Paul and is due by Friday." The communication is linked back to a piece of work, such as a task that is to be fulfilled at the end of the day. By having communication occur inside a task manager, decisions are made quicker and work happens faster. Productivity and efficiency increases, because your communication is alongside your work.

People don't have a task manager with email. There's no way of seeing who's doing what. Everyone must interpret the email, decide who's doing what, and you must guess about what to do.

You may work with outside contractors. Invite them into your Asana account. Let's say that contractor doesn't use Asana every day. They can enable email notifications and get notified about tasks and messages you send. You may be working inside Asana every day, and you don't want those notifications. Deal with those updates natively in Asana.

Asana is a wonderful tool to manage clients. Invite a client into your account to show the project you setup, tasks that need completing, and specific tasks you need from that client. Often, client work is slowed down waiting on information from that client.

If you ask for a response from a client via email, that request could get lost, or the client may forget about it. It's low priority and not their work. After a week, they ask you, "What's the status on this project?" Your response: "I'm waiting on you." Miscommunication.

Asana allows you to invite that client into your system to show the project and timeline. That will illustrate that the client needs to deliver one task, which will allow you to complete many other tasks. Everyone can easily see what's slowing the project down.

It can be a challenge to get everyone onboard with a tool, including Asana.

Step #1: **Reorganize and structure the account** in the best way for the business, based on the processes and the projects your people are managing. Asana begins as a blank slate. Creating the best structure can be a challenge.

Do you use projects? Tasks? Sub-tasks? How do you manage clients? Many times, business owners setup too many projects. They don't take advantage of Asana properly. When you have too many projects, it becomes difficult to see who's doing what. Get it all organized before you bring the team in. If you don't understand what you're setting up, what hope does your team have?

Step #2: In preparation for onboarding your team, consider the **rules and best practices** that govern how you'll use Asana. When do we communicate in Slack versus Asana? Who assigns tasks to whom? Who marks tasks complete? How will we use due dates?

Example: If I assign a task to you, then you complete that task... do I mark it as complete, or do you? Unless you define upfront that the person receiving the task is responsible for marking it as complete, several incomplete tasks may pile up.

Make formal decisions around those little things. How will we use this tool?

Step #3: Plan a **test roll-out** with a small team or department. Get a few people in your organization onboard. Get feedback before moving onto a larger team.

If you run a small to medium sized team, you could meet with everyone and demonstrate the basics:

- How the system is setup.

- The agreed upon rules everyone will follow.

- Where to find projects.

- Introduce key features.

Have an internal Asana champion, who's great at learning new tools, who can lead that training, keep the account organized, answer questions from the team, and be the Asana "guru."

After setting up those best practices, roll it out to your team. Monitor progress to see how people use it. Make changes to the structure and rules based on real-life usage you observe. It's an ongoing process. You won't get the structure perfected out of the gate. Evolve as you go.

Pipedrive is a sales Customer Relationship Management tool. It plays in the same sandbox as Salesforce, Zoho, Keap by InfusionSoft, and HubSpot, to some extent. Use it to manage and track the leads and clients you're selling to. Every CRM is different, for example, InfusionSoft is designed to manage thousands of leads at once, including marketing automation. Pipedrive is better geared for one-on-one sales.

For example, in my consulting business, I have 20-30 leads in my pipeline: people who have approached me for possible consulting. Some leads are booked for a meeting, some have proposals, some have confirmed their interest, and others are pending payment. I can create rules for different stages.

Pipedrive makes it easy to see who's at which stage of that journey. It's not for tracking and managing thousands of leads. It's a direct sales tool, and a task manager. It has activity management built-in.

Someone approaches you for consulting. Create a deal. Assign activities to that deal so you know when to follow up or write a proposal. Track engagements with that client. When you call them on the phone, log that call and write notes.

Pipedrive is geared for sales, specifically, the activities you complete as you move deals through stages. This feeds into Pipedrive's reports, which gives information about your sales process. Because of these reports, I know my conversion rate on deals is about 50 percent. Half the people who approach me will work with me.

Pipedrive gives you that information clearly. It shows your conversion rates at different stages. I usually see a big drop off after the "proposal sent" stage. I often lose potential clients after sending a proposal. The information it provides about my sales process is incredibly valuable.

Pipedrive is geared towards sales. It's a fantastic tool. Once your team begins using it, assign deals to sales people. You'll see who closes the most deals, and who does the most work -- activities. Stay on top of the potential leads and clients you want to work with, in one place.

Next Steps

1. What systems and processes does your business currently have in place for task management?

2. Have you begun using Asana yourself before your other team members begin using it?

3. Which team member will function as the Champion to answer questions?

4. What is the plan for your test roll-out?

Paul's Contact Information

- PaulMinors.com (official site)

Chapter 17: Become Your Best Self and Discover Your Aligned Life Roadmap by River Easter

River Easter is a catalyst who helps you discover "the genius inside you." She's more than your average life coach. Her vast toolbox includes more than 25 years of neuroscience, smartcuts and paradigm-busting processes. She has a Master's in

Organization Development, and she's a Certified Life Mastery Consultant. Her genius is part alchemy, part science and part consciousness hacking. We're about to discover about River's inspiring workshops and her transformational high touch coaching programs, and we're about to help you transition from surviving to thriving with ease.

I've always been interested in how to become the best person that I am deep down. I want that for you as well. I've studied human nature my entire life. I have a Master's in Organization Development, which is about how to transform organizations to creating environments that thrive on a technical and social level.

I became aware of the patterns I was stuck in. For example, I found myself in a relationship that wasn't working out. I moved into another relationship, and experienced the same results.

Has something similar happened to you? Let's say you were unsatisfied with a job. You moved to a new job, and still found yourself unhappy and stuck.

I noticed my own negative thoughts, paradigms, and mental models. I observed limiting beliefs and unhelpful thoughts, such as, "Life is hard and then you die." Or, "You have to struggle to make money." "I'm not good enough." I was stuck but didn't know how to change. I was frustrated because I couldn't figure it out. I had incredible training, but no idea how to apply it to transform my own life.

Wherever you go, there you are. We have been trained to manipulate our circumstances. We become stuck in the habit of thinking, "If only THIS changes, I'll be ready and happy." In reality, it's the opposite. Start within yourself.

A common mistake: squirrel syndrome. Lack of focus and follow through. You're distracted by shiny objects. You jump from one thing to the next.

Once I was introduced to the system that allowed me to get results and transform my pattern, it completely shifted everything. **That system is: clarity, focus, and action.**

Our world is designed to distract us. Being distracted is a method of procrastination. It's temporary relief of an inner fear. These unconscious fears produce anxiety.

The thoughts you think create chemical responses in your body. Neuroscience links your thoughts with physical changes in your brain. If you're constantly stressed and have worry or self-doubt, it changes your brain over time.

Pay attention to your thoughts. Being mindful is important. Instead of allowing your thoughts to terrorize you, rewire these reactionary emotional loops.

Switch or pivot your thoughts by expressing gratitude. Example: "I'm worried. What can I think about instead of worrying?" Worrying doesn't get you anywhere except in a more stressed out position.

A recent client was regretting a decision. "I made the wrong decision. That was a wrong thing to do." That client realized that no matter what decision they made, it became a regret.

We have 70,000 thoughts per day. Most thoughts are ones we've thought before, because our brain is designed to save energy. It takes a lot of energy to think, so your brain relies on automatic responses.

Mindfulness is awareness of your thoughts and feelings without judgment. Learning to think without judgment is the first step.

The second step: noticing where the regret train is taking you. I helped my client unpack these reactionary emotional loops. She had "regret" issues. She could choose a different thought in that moment instead of riding the regret train.

My client had spent a ton of money on a property. Her stress level was high, but she was able to focus on her vision. Why had she done it? What did she love about it? She needed to trust that her original decision and intuition were correct. It worked out because she's in a great financial place. However, she had the fear she was going to be homeless. She couldn't trust herself.

Start small. Notice what you're thinking, without judgment, and pivot to something more aligned with the vision for yourself, more aligned with the truth about you.

Notice your thoughts and feelings. Do you have low vibrational thoughts? Fear, worry, self-doubt, anger, frustration? You're not alone. This is common with business owners.

Procrastination usually stems from some inner fear. Why aren't you making those important phone calls? Why aren't you moving the needle in your business? The root cause could be fear of rejection, fear of performance, fear of not being good enough.

It could be fear of failure or fear of success.

"What if I am too successful? Will I lose my freedom?" If I'm in the state of suffering, how can I move into a state of expansion and possibility? Gratitude is an easy pivot to get there.

Another issue: the hamster wheel. Many business owners lack clarity and commitment. Failure to make up one's mind, lack of clarity and desire, leaving room for backing out at the last minute. One foot in and one foot out. They haven't made their decision and they don't have clear goals.

They're not breaking the endgame down into a 6 to 12 month goal. There's lack of clarity plus lack of commitment. That's why I developed "the roadmap." It's a framework that helps you figure out what you love to do.

Start with a three-year goal. Ask yourself, "What would I love?" Start small. Don't let limiting beliefs prevent you from acting.

You can always call me. I have a breakthrough session that gets you clear about your goals. You'll uncover hidden challenges and create an action plan. Make a vision board, be your own counsel, listen to your intuition, develop a plan of action and stick to it.

Write down your goals. Make a commitment to take action on them no matter what. Your fears will emerge, you'll procrastinate, and try to talk yourself out of it, or delay yourself.

Get clear about what you love to do. Develop a plan of action and get support. It takes 220 days to rewire a neuropathway. You're rewiring your brain from old patterns into new ones that are in harmony with you. Many times, people say, "I'm unsatisfied because I don't have this or I don't have that. When I have THAT, things will be better." Change your world right now.

There's more going on in life than what meets the eye. Our brains are goal achieving machines. We process 400 billion bits of information per nanosecond, but only perceive a small portion because we don't have the bandwidth to perceive that consciously.

When you write down your goals and vision, and it's based on what you love, you travel into a land of your own intuition because you're following your own path.

Writing it down is your way of saying something to the universe. Your brain thinks, "We'll figure this out." You've incorporated a huge amount of brain capacity to solving a problem. Previously, you lacked a clear plan. This gets you clear.

This is based on research. When you write your goal or vision down, you increase your chances of achieving it by 42 percent.

When we live in the land of suffering, we are unhooked from creativity, from inspired action. Use gratitude to move into a state of higher frequency. That will make you feel better, and you'll be able to make new connections that were not visible before.

When I'm in the land of suffering, I can't see my way out of a wet paper bag. I believe that I have no friends and no talents. We've all been there. We want to stay in bed, not make phone calls, avoid the things real business people do.

Moving energy into your walk increases your energy and gratitude.

I write a gratitude list every morning. I write, "I'm grateful that I'm alive, and that I get to feel the emotions I'm feeling today. I'm grateful for my health." I say ten gratitudes every day, which change over time.

It's no coincidence you're taking in this information. You have a purpose, and that will unfold through the things you desire. Everyone has a different vision. Create that roadmap.

Remember, you'll increase your odds by 42 percent by getting your clear goals in writing. If more people do what they love to do, that are aligned with who they are, and why they're here, the world will be a much better place to live in.

I believe in you. You can become the person you want to be.

Next Steps

1. What negative thoughts and feelings do you have on a recurring basis that hold you back?

2. What fears do you need to overcome?

3. What's your morning routine? Does it include meditation and mindfulness?

4. What is your 6 to 12 month goal?

River's Contact Information

- YourAlignedLifeRoadmap.com (free resource, create a powerful vision to hit your goals)

- RiverEaster.com (official site)

Conclusion

We would like to thank you for finishing the *Marketer of the Day* book. What should you do now?

1. Take some personal inventory and ask yourself which chapter, which personal story in this book, stuck with you the most. Quickly re-read that chapter!

2. Think about two or three quick takeaways or tips that you found the most powerful. This could be a mind-hack, business technique, way of being organized, or perspective. What is it?

3. Out of everything you learned from this book, what is the #1 thing you can take action on within the next 30 days?

4. Leave a quick (and honest) review of this book at MarketerOfTheDay.com/amazon. We greatly appreciate it.

5. Listen and subscribe to our podcast at MarketerOfTheDay.com. You'll love it!

6. Contact at least one of the authors in this book to thank them for their advice, ask a quick question, or inquire about their coaching services.

If you enjoyed what you learned and want more books like this, send a thank you email to Robert Plank at robert@robertplank.com.

www.ingramcontent.com/pod-product-compliance
Lightning Source LLC
Chambersburg PA
CBHW031628210526
45464CB00004B/1795